30-Day Indian Keto Recipes

RIMA PAI is an engineer based in Silicon Valley in the United States. With a high-profile job and fast-paced life with two kids, she had always ignored her health. As the years went by, she discovered that her weight kept fluctuating and she'd developed certain medical conditions. Finally, she decided that it was time to take charge and that's when she heard about the Keto diet through a friend and discovered its health benefits while losing weight! The only hurdle was that everywhere she looked, she could only find Western recipes—and she loved her Indian desi food. That's when the creative spark came to light and she had fun creating mouth-watering Indian recipes that adhered to the diet. This was one diet which she just loved being on! And, to add to that, she was amazed to see the health benefits it had. She vowed to share her work with as many Indians as possible and this book is her attempt at it.

30-Day Indian Keto Recipes

Lose Weight with Delicious Indian Keto Food

RIMA PAI

Photographs
RANJANA YADAV

First published by Westland Publications Private Limited in 2019

1st Floor, A Block, East Wing, Plot No. 40, SP Infocity, Dr MGR Salai, Perungudi, Kandanchavadi, Chennai 600096

Westland and the Westland logo are the trademarks of Westland Publications Private Limited, or its affiliates.

Copyright © Deepa Shenoy, Salil Khamkar, 2019
Photographs copyright © Ranjana Yadav, 2019

ISBN: 9789388754552

Typeset by Jojy Philip, New Delhi 110 015

For M,
for standing by me, through thick and thin,
literally and figuratively

Contents

SNACKS AND SIDES

DESSERTS

My Very Own Keto Story

I was never skinny but I wasn't too fat either. I was just a chubby teenager, the kind people called cute. Cute is a not a bad adjective when you are a teenager but as I grew older and wiser, I realised that the chubbiness was not exactly going away or paving way for different adjectives like attractive, fit, active or even energetic.

I went through the usual rites of passage like other Indian women. I finished my education, started working, got married, had two children and for a long time, life centred around children, husband, home and work.

My health, I realised, had somehow taken a backseat. My weight, especially after my second child, was not exactly ideal and I was not happy about how my clothes fit. I have never been one to 'diet', I mean I love food. I spend a fair amount of time thinking about it, planning meals, talking to friends about restaurants and a lot of my fond memories are about food. I knew giving up food and starving myself was not how it was going to pan out. It would have probably meant more waking hours spent anxiously thinking about my next meal! Until one day in the middle of a conversation with a friend, I heard the term 'Keto diet' for the very first time. My friend mentioned how it allowed you to eat almost all the food groups unlike some restrictive diets, kept you fuller for a long time and the best part of all, it made you lose weight. I was sceptical at first, but as I researched more about Keto, I realised how it had become a way of life to certain people and how great it made them feel. I was convinced that it was worth trying. It made complete sense to cut out processed foods and sugar as we have known for a long time that they aren't good for health. I was worried if I'd be able to give up some of my favourites like bread and pasta or if I would have to give up eating good old desi ghar ka khaana. I decided to give it a shot for a month, like a really good shot and to my surprise, I started losing weight. I started going for walks as well and soon, I felt better, my clothes fit better and I figured out that I could enjoy a lot of my regular meals with some minor tweaking.

This book was created to help others like me, to plan and make simple home-cooked meals. There is no need for fancy or expensive ingredients. You can use the ingredients easily available in most of our homes. All you need is the will to see a healthier and a fitter you and make this a way of life.

For those of you who were kind enough to buy the first e-book, I will forever be grateful. I learnt a lot while writing it and I realised I made some mistakes too. This new upgraded book has your suggestions and recommendations and I hope it is a step in the right direction for those of you who want to start their own Keto journey and sustain it.

As with any other diet, please make sure to discuss your diet with your doctor or a health professional, especially if you have any medical conditions and are on medication.

Introduction to Keto

A Ketogenic diet or a Keto diet is a low-carb, high-fat diet that is moderate in proteins.

The diet involves reducing carbohydrate intake to a substantially low level and replacing it with fat so that the body shifts its metabolism to burn fat for fuel rather than carbohydrates. This reduction puts the body in the metabolic state that is known as ketosis.

When the body is in a ketosis state, it starts burning fat for fuel and forces the liver to convert fat into ketones which also supplies the energy to the brain.

A Ketogenic diet can cause a drastic reduction in blood sugar and insulin levels and hence has numerous health benefits and is often responsible for reversing Type 2 diabetes.

In general, when we are consuming food that is high in carbs, our body produces glucose and insulin. Glucose is the easiest molecule that can be used as energy and hence it works as the primary energy source. Glucose is needed in the creation of ATP (an energy molecule) which fuels and maintains our bodies.

Insulin is produced by the body to process the glucose in the blood stream. It helps control the blood glucose level by signaling the liver, muscle and fat cells to take the glucose directly from the bloodstream for energy.

In case the body's energy levels are met, a portion of the excess glucose is stored by the liver as glycogen. Up to five per cent of the liver's mass can be stored as glycogen. In this case, since glucose is being used as the fundamental source of energy, fats are not need and hence are stored in the body.

There are two main processes that happen when your body uses glucose if it doesn't need it:

- **Glycogenesis:** Excess glucose will be converted to glycogen, and stored in your liver and muscles. Estimates show that only about half of your daily energy can be stored as glycogen.
- **Lipogenesis:** If there's already enough glycogen in your muscles and liver, any extra glucose will be converted into fats and stored. That is why someone could be putting on weight since the body is consuming lesser energy as compared to what is being produced through the consumption of food.

When one lowers the source of carbs, the body automatically shifts into a state known as Ketosis. The ketosis state is also triggered when one is fasting and is in fact one of the fastest ways to put the body in the ketosis state. Some religions and cultures promote fasting for precisely this reason. Unfortunately, sometimes this leads to eating food that is not always healthy.

But obviously, it's not possible to fast forever. A low-carb or Keto diet, on the other hand, can be eaten on a regular basis and results in ketosis. It has many benefits of fasting—including weight loss—without having to fast.

What Is Ketosis?

When the body is in a ketosis state, it produces substitute fuel molecules called ketones and which is where the word 'Keto' in the Keto diet comes from. Ketones provide fuel to the body when glucose or blood sugar is in short supply.

These ketones are produced when one is on a low-carb diet. It is important to note that a Keto diet is a low-carb, high-fat and moderate-protein diet. Excess protein can easily be converted into blood sugar and in turn, stored as fat which pulls the body out of the ketosis mode.

Ketosis is an everyday process of the body, regardless of the number of carbs you eat. Your body can adapt very well, processing different types of nutrients into the fuels it requires. Proteins, fats and carbs can all be processed for use. Eating a low-carb, high-fat diet just ramps up this process and is a normal and safe chemical reaction.

These ketones (acetoacetate) are created when the body breaks down fats, creating fatty acids which are burned off in the liver in a process called betaoxidation. The result of this process is the creation of 2 other ketones (BHB and acetone) which are used as fuel by the muscles and the brain.

When the body is in ketosis, it becomes easy to access fat reserves which help to burn existing stored fat as energy, helping to make one's body a 'fat burning machine'. Another added advantage of the process is that the insulin levels also drop. This is obviously great if you're trying to lose weight!

Ketosis is an amazing state to be in. In fact, certain studies show that the body and the brain prefer using ketones rather than glucose and run seventy per cent more efficiently.

How Does Your Body Handle This Change?

Since the human body is used to the simple process of breaking down carbohydrates into glucose and using it as energy, over time, the body builds up an arsenal of enzymes ready for energy conversion, and only a few enzymes for dealing with fats which it mostly stores. Since the body must suddenly deal with the lack of glucose and increase in fats, it means that it will start creating a new supply of enzymes.

As the body gets into a ketogenic state, it will naturally use what's left of the glucose in the blood stream. It will also deplete the glycogen stores in the muscles which can cause a lack of energy, and a general lethargy. In the first few weeks, many people report:

- Headaches
- Mental fogginess
- Flu-like symptoms (known as the Keto flu)
- Dizziness

Often, this is the result of electrolytes being flushed out, as ketosis has a diuretic effect. Make sure to drink plenty of water and keep up your sodium intake through salt. This will increase water retention and replenish the electrolytes.

You can find out the ketosis levels in your body by testing for Ketones in your blood or urine by using Keto sticks. Some blood sugar meters can also measure ketones in your blood. Be careful because extremely high levels of ketones are dangerous.

Ketones Are Brain Fuel

The brain can easily burn carbs when they are consumed, although if the carb consumption is much lower, ketones can be used up instead.

This is a necessary function for basic survival. As the body can only store carbs for a day or two, the brain would quickly shut down after a couple of days without food. Alternatively, it would quickly have to convert our muscle protein into glucose which can be an inefficient process to keep the brain in a working condition.

Fortunately, our bodies have evolved to be smarter than that. Normally we have fat stores that last so that we can survive for months without food. Ketosis is how the body makes sure that the brain can run on those fat stores too.

Bottom line: We do not need to eat any carbs at all. The brain can happily run on fat.

Many people report that they feel more energised and focused when the brain gets to run on ketones made from fat. And it certainly speeds up fat loss if you're trying to lose weight.

Benefits of Ketosis

1) Elimination of Cravings:

Most people report that hunger is the worst side effect of dieting as it leads to cravings and in turn, makes dieting a high stress mental game. It also causes feelings of guilt when one ends up eating more that the controlled portions.

This is one of the main reasons why many people feel miserable and eventually give up on their diets.

One of the best things about following a Ketogenic diet is that it leads to an automatic reduction in appetite and feeling of satiation.

The studies consistently show that when people cut carbs and eat more fat and protein, they end up eating fewer calories.

2) Keto Diet Leads to More Weight Loss

Studies show that people on only low-carb diets lose more weight, faster, than people on low-fat diet, even when the low-fat dieters are actively restricting calories.

One of the reasons for this is that low-carb diets tend to get rid of excess water from the body. Because they lower insulin levels, the kidneys start shedding excess sodium, leading to rapid weight loss in the first week or two.

Studies comparing the Keto diet with other traditional diets have shown that people end up losing two to three times more weight while following the Keto diet as compared to others, without feeling constantly hungry!

3) Faster Reduction of Belly Fat

Not all fat in the body is the same. It's where that fat is stored that determines how it will affect our health and risk of disease. Fat can be categorised as subcutaneous fat (under the skin) and visceral fat (in the abdominal cavity).

This visceral fat is the fat that tends to lodge around the organs and can cause inflammation, insulin resistance and metabolic dysfunction. The Keto diet is very effective at reducing this harmful abdominal fat. Not only does the Ketogenic diet promote faster fat loss compared to low-fat diets, a big proportion of that fat comes from the visceral fat within the abdomen. Over time, this leads to a drastically reduced risk of heart disease and Type 2 diabetes.

4) Reduction in Triglycerides

Triglycerides are fat molecules and elevated trigyceride levels in the blood after an overnight fast is an indicator of being at high risk for heart disease.

One of the main drivers of elevated triglycerides is carbohydrate consumption, especially the simple sugar-fructose.

When people cut carbs, they tend to have a very dramatic reduction in blood triglycerides.

5) Increased Levels Of Good Cholesterol (HDL)

High Density Lipoprotein (HDL) is often called the 'good' cholesterol. HDL and LDL refer to the lipoproteins that carry cholesterol around in the blood. While LDL carries cholesterol from the liver and to the rest of the body, HDL carries cholesterol away from the body and to the liver, where it can be reused or excreted.

It is well known that the higher your levels of HDL, the lower your risk of heart disease will be.

One of the best ways to increase HDL levels is to eat fat and a Keto diet includes a lot of fat.

While on the Keto diet, the HDL levels increase dramatically whereas they tend to increase only moderately or even go down on low-fat diets.

The Triglycerides: HDL ratio is another strong predictor of heart disease risk. The higher it is, the greater your risk of heart disease is. By lowering triglycerides and raising HDL levels, low-carb diets lead to a major improvement in this ratio.

6) Reduction in Blood Sugar and Insulin Levels

When we eat carbs, they are broken down into simple sugars (mostly glucose) in the digestive tract. From there, they enter the bloodstream and elevate blood sugar levels. Because high blood sugar level is toxic, the body responds with a hormone called insulin, which tells the cells to bring the glucose into the cells to start burning or storing it. For people who are healthy, the quick insulin response tends to minimise the blood sugar spike to prevent it from harming us.

However, many people have major problems with this process. They have insulin resistance, which means that the cells don't 'see' the insulin and therefore, it is harder for the body to bring the blood sugar into the cells. This can lead to a disease called Type 2 diabetes, when the body fails to secrete enough insulin to lower the blood sugar after meals. This disease is very rampant today, afflicting about 300 million people worldwide.

There is a very simple solution to this problem. By cutting carbohydrates, you remove the need for all that insulin. Both blood sugars and insulin levels reduce substantially. One study on patients with Type 2 diabetes claimed that 95.2 per cent of them had managed to reduce or eliminate their glucose-lowering medication within six months. If you are currently on blood sugar lowering medication, then talk to your doctor before making changes to your carbohydrate intake because your dosage may need to be adjusted to prevent hypoglycemia.

7) Blood Pressure Level Reduction

Elevated blood pressure (hypertension) can lead to heart disease, stroke, kidney failure and many other diseases.

Low-carb diets are an effective way to reduce blood pressure, which should lead to a reduced risk of these diseases and help you live longer.

8) Most Effective Treatment against Metabolic Syndrome

The metabolic syndrome is a medical condition that is highly associated with the risk of diabetes and heart disease.

Symptoms of this syndrome include:

- Abdominal obesity
- Elevated blood pressure
- Elevated fasting blood sugar levels
- High triglycerides
- Low HDL levels

All these symptoms typically improve on a Keto diet.

Side Effects of the Keto Diet

Although the Ketogenic diet is safe for healthy people, there may be some initial side effects while the body adapts to the new diet.

This is often referred to as 'Keto flu' and is usually over within a few days.

Keto flu includes a drop in energy and mental function, sleep issues, nausea, digestive discomfort and decreased performance during exercise.

To minimise this, you can try a regular low-carb diet for the first few weeks. This may teach your body to burn more fat before you completely eliminate carbs.

A Ketogenic diet can also change the water and mineral balance of your body, so adding extra salt to your meals or taking mineral supplements can help. It is extremely important to keep the body well-hydrated at all times and you should aim to drink at least two to three litres of water every day.

For minerals, try taking 3,000–4,000 mg of sodium, 1,000 mg of potassium and 300 mg of magnesium per day to minimise side effects.

In the beginning, it is important to eat till you feel full and avoid any restrictions on calories. This diet usually causes weight loss without any intentional calorific restriction.

What to Eat and What to Avoid on Keto?

There is a great deal of information on the internet about what can be eaten and what can be avoided on a Ketogenic diet. Being aware of what you put into your body is extremely important. A lot of us have probably experienced first-hand what mindless eating can do. This simple guide should help you determine what can be used while cooking up a meal or while rustling up a snack. It will also help when you have to eat out so you can make informed choices.

Since Keto is a high-fat, moderate-protein and low-carb diet, make sure to include those components appropriately.

FATS

Make sure to eat:
1. Saturated fats like butter, ghee and coconut oil.

2. Monounsaturated fats like olive oil and avocado oil. You can use extra virgin olive oil for dressing up salads or to finish up a meal.

3. Polyunsaturated fats should be consumed only if they are naturally present in ingredients like fish and seafood.

Steer clear of:
1. Trans fats like hydrogenated oils and refined oils like sunflower, canola and margarine.

PROTEIN

Make sure to eat:

1. Poultry like chicken, duck and quail. You can also eat organ meats like heart, liver and kidneys.

2. Eggs.

3. Fish that is locally available like mackerels/bangda, surmai/sear/kingfish, tuna, salmon, rawas/Indian salmon, pomfret, sardines.

4. Shellfish in the form of prawns, mussels, shellfish, lobster, squid, crab.

5. Animal protein from mutton, beef, pork, ham, turkey, veal, bacon and sausages. Organ meats like heart, liver and kidneys can be consumed as well.

Steer clear of:

1. Cured meats with added sugar.

2. Pulses like dals, chana, rajma and beans.

DAIRY

Make sure to eat:

1. Full-fat dairy products like full-fat dahi/yoghurt, paneer, fresh cream, heavy whipped cream, sour cream, cream cheese, full-fat Greek yoghurt.

2. Cheese in the form of cheddar, mozzarella, parmesan, ricotta, feta, Colby, gouda, Monterey Jack, mascarpone.

3. Spreads like full-fat mayonnaise.

Steer clear of:

1. Dairy products like full-fat milk, store-bought mithai and sweets, sweetened khoya, and products that claim to be low fat but are filled with binders.

FRUITS AND VEGETABLES

Make sure to eat:

1. Leafy greens and vegetables like palak/spinach, methi/fenugreek, moringa/drumstick leaves, broccoli, cauliflower, cabbage, green beans, lauki, lettuce, cucumber, zucchini, celery, asparagus.

2. Vegetables like brinjal/brinjal, mushrooms, garlic, ginger, onions, bhindi/lady's finger and tomatoes are to be consumed in moderation.

3. Fruits for most part contain a lot of sugar so berries like strawberries are to be consumed moderately. Use avocados since they are full of good fats. Citrus fruits like lemon and orange are best used for dressing up salads and for flavouring meats and fish. Also, to be used while making flavoured water or drinks.

Steer clear of:

1. Vegetables like potatoes, peas, corn, carrots.

2. Fruits like bananas, mangoes, papaya, watermelons, peaches, grapes, pomegranates.

NUTS AND SEEDS

Make sure to eat:

1. Low-carb nuts like macadamia nuts and pecans, chia, pumpkin, sesame seeds.

2. Moderate carb nuts like almonds, walnuts and peanuts.

Steer clear of:

1. Heavy carb nuts like cashews and pistachios.

FLOURS AND GRAINS

Make sure to eat:

1. Flours like coconut flour, almond flour, flaxseed flour and soy flour, unsweetened desiccated coconut, psyllium husk.

Steer clear of:
1. Flours like rice flour, wheat flour, besan, corn, rajgira, bajra, jowar, rava and avoid products made from them.
2. Grains like oats, rajgira, rice, quinoa.

SPICES, SEASONINGS, CONDIMENTS, SAUCES, and SWEETENERS

Make sure to eat:
1. Spices like sea salt, haldi/turmeric, chilli powder, jeera/cumin, cayenne, cinnamon/dalchini, cloves/laung, cardamom/elaichi, mustard/rai.
2. Seasonings like garam masala, chaat masala, jaljeera, coriander leaves/kothimir/hara dhania, Italian seasoning, basil, oregano, thyme, parsley.
3. Condiments like olives, mustard, apple cider vinegar, ketchup with no sugar.
4. Sauces like soya sauce, green chilli and red chilli sauces without sugar, sriracha and Worcestershire sauce.
5. Sweeteners available as Stevia, Erythritol, Xylitol.

Steer clear of:
1. Condiments and sauces which contain sugar and MSG.
2. Artificial sweeteners.

DRINKS AND BEVERAGES

Make sure to drink and use:
1. Liquids like water, broths, soups without sugar and use the right ingredients, flavoured waters, smoothies made with Keto friendly ingredients, unsweetened almond and coconut milk, coffee, green tea.

Steer clear of:
1. Fresh fruit juices of all kinds since they are high in sugar.
2. Milk, sodas, diet sodas, alcohol.
3. Cocktails and Mocktails.

MISCELLANEOUS

Make sure to use:
1. Unsweetened cocoa powder, dark chocolate, whey protein powder (90 per cent and above).

Steer clear of:
1. Processed foods like breads, pasta, noodles, store-bought sweets and desserts.

How to Calculate Your Daily Macros

Follow the link below to calculate your personal macros.
    https://keto-calculator.ankerl.com

Note:
For those recipes where the protein content is lower, and you need more protein to meet your daily macros, you can consume protein powder to supplement your protein needs.

Intermittent Fasting

Intermittent Fasting or IF as it is popularly called is eating according to a fixed schedule and having a fixed period of fasting. This strategy doesn't get into what foods are suitable but essentially only talks about the time period where the body remains in a state of fasting. IF has its followers irrespective of the diet they follow. It's up to an individual to choose to integrate it into their lifestyles. However, when combined with a Ketogenic diet, IF has been found to be very beneficial.

Common IF strategies include having a daily sixteen-hour fast (called as the fasting window) and eating in an eight-hour window (called as the feeding window). The sixteen hours may sound like a lot, but it could simply mean that you skip breakfast. A typical IF strategy is to finish dinner by 8 p.m. and directly have lunch the next day at noon. This gives a sixteen-hour fasting window and an eight-hour window from 12 p.m. to 8 p.m. where one can consume other meals.

For some users, intermittent fasting simply means not having breakfast and having half a litre of water and getting on with their day. This strategy is one of the best ways to get rid of fat and requires only a slight shift in habit—one that is very easy to follow once you get started.

So what does fasting do to our bodies? Fasting has been practiced for a long time and is recommended by several cultures across the world. There definitely has to be some science behind a practice that is still prevalent even in today's times.

So let's see what happens during the intermittent fast.

Imagine we have two kinds of energy storage systems in our body. One is short term and the other is long term. The short term storage system is the glycogen stored in the liver. This system can be quickly mobilised to meet our sudden need of energy. The long term storage system is the adipose tissue or the fat cells. So after consuming our meals, whenever the short term storage system is full, we start storing in the fat cells or the long term storage.

This long term energy storage system can only be used if the short term storage system has been exhausted. So you can imagine that if we constantly keep consuming food and sending it to the short term storage system in our body, we are never giving our bodies the chance to tap into the energy stored in the long term storage system.

Multiple studies that have been done in this space have shown that on the twelve-hour fasting mark, the short term energy storage system in our body is completely depleted. On its depletion, our body starts tapping in the long term energy storage system that is the fat in our body. So even if you fast for twelve hours, you get the same benefit. However, the peak of this benefit is around the sixteen-hour mark. This is based on a study of averages. If someone has more secondary storage reserves then it might take them more time to access this energy reserve.

One of the main reason why intermittent fasting is very popular is that helps you eat less. When people say that they aren't getting any benefit out of this practice, it is because during the feeding window, they end up binge eating, consuming extra food and filling up their long term storage with more energy than what they need during the fasting window.

Studies have shown that the most common benefits of intermittent fasting have been:

• Fat loss
• Reduction of bad cholesterol (LDL Cholesterol)
• Decrease in levels of triglycerides

- Reduction of fasting insulin levels
- Help in maintaining muscle mass
- Decrease in hunger
- Reduced levels of inflammation
- Reduced levels of blood sugar

Some studies have shown that doing the intermittent fast is directly related to human longevity since the cells initiate a cellular repair process during the fasting state.

For these reasons, intermittent fasting is often the ultimate hack. It is a simple strategy that can improve health. It has had a significant impact for those who have tried it.

But is it for everyone? Definitely not if you are underweight, or have an eating disorder. As with all lifestyle changes, please consult with your physician if you have any ongoing medical conditions or take any medication.

One way to find out if this strategy is for you is to try it out! If you want to get started with Intermittent Fasting, get free access to our 7-day Intermittent Fasting Challenge and other bonus material at https://www.ketomonk.com/bonus.

MAINS

Vegetable Upma

Upma or upittu is a popular breakfast and tiffin dish. On busy mornings, I am more than happy to make this for lunch too. You can skip the vegetables completely if you want or add them as per your macros.

Ingredients

2 cups riced cauliflower
½ cup finely chopped onions
¼ cup finely chopped tomatoes (skip this if you dislike tomatoes in your upma)
¼ cup chopped and parboiled green beans
¼ cup chopped green bell peppers or capsicum
2 tbsp. ghee
1 tsp. mustard seeds
Sprig of curry leaves
1 tsp. finely chopped ginger
2–3 green slit green chillies
½ tsp. turmeric powder
1 tsp. lemon juice
1 tbsp. finely chopped fresh coriander leaves
1 tbsp. fresh grated coconut
Salt to taste

Bringing everything together

1. Heat the ghee in a thick-bottomed pan, when it melts, add the mustard seeds and let them splutter.

2. Add the green chillies, curry leaves and ginger. Fry for a minute and then add the onions.

3. Fry the onions till they turn translucent and soften and then add the tomatoes.

4. Once the tomatoes soften, add the chopped bell peppers and sauté for a couple of minutes. Next, add the beans and mix everything together. Cook for a couple of minutes.

5. Add the turmeric powder and enough salt and then the riced cauliflower.

6. Stir everything well, sprinkle some water to cook the cauliflower and cover the pan. Check intermittently to make sure the upma doesn't stick to the pan.

7. After 8–10 minutes, check and cook until the cauliflower is tender and done.

8. Add the lemon juice and adjust salt as needed. Garnish with fresh coriander leaves and grated coconut. Mix everything well and serve.

Nutritional Information Per Serving
Serving Size – 2

Amount Per Serving
Calories 210
Total Fat 18 g
Total Carbohydrate 8 g
Protein 3 g

Pav Bhaaji

This is probably one quintessential street food favourite and a lot of us will always have fond memories of scarfing down loaves of buttered pav with butter laden bright red bhaaji! Replacing carb heavy potatoes with cauliflower and a few other Keto friendly ingredients is all it will take to make your pav bhaaji Ketogenic and enjoyable as well.

Ingredients

500 gms. cauliflower (cut into big florets)

100 gms. chopped french beans

100 gms. chopped cabbage

200 gms. salted butter

¾ cup finely chopped onions

¾ cup finely chopped tomatoes

½ cup finely chopped bell peppers or capsicum

1 tbsp. minced garlic

2 tsp. red chilli powder

1 tbsp. pav bhaaji masala

2 tbsp. finely chopped fresh coriander leaves or cilantro

1 small lemon cut into quarters

Salt to taste

Bringing everything together

1. Pressure cook the cauliflower, french beans and chopped cabbage with very little water until soft. Alternatively, you can steam them until they are really soft. Once done and cooled slightly, mash them together using a potato masher or the back of your ladle until the vegetables are all blended well and soft.

2. Heat up a pan and add about 100 gms of butter. Once it melts, add the onions and cook for a couple of minutes. At this point add the minced garlic and keep stirring until the onions are translucent and the garlic doesn't smell raw anymore.

3. Add the chopped tomatoes and cook until they are soft and mushy.

4. Add the red chilli powder and pav bhaaji masala and fry for a minute.

5. Add the chopped bell peppers and fry for 2–3 minutes and then add the cooked vegetables and blend everything well together.

6. Add another 50 gms of butter, salt to taste and water. Cover and cook for another 10–12 minutes. Keep stirring in between.

7. Serve it with Keto bread toasted in butter after topping the bhaaji with the remaining butter, finely chopped fresh coriander and some lemon juice.

Nutritional Information Per Serving
Serving Size – 4

Amount Per Serving
Calories 475
Total Fat 42 g
Total Carbohydrate 13 g
Protein 5 g

Cauliflower Tehri

A tehri is similar to pulao which is made with rice and vegetables like potatoes, peas and carrots. In this version, we will use cauliflower rice as the base and vegetables like mushrooms, bell peppers and paneer. You can use the vegetables you like and feel free to skip the ones that you don't. I also add methi or fresh fenugreek leaves and spinach if I have them on hand.

Ingredients

- 2 cups riced cauliflower
- 1/2 cup sliced onions
- ¼ cup chopped tomatoes
- ½ cup each of sliced bell peppers or capsicum and mushrooms
- ½ cup of paneer cubes pan roasted in some ghee
- 2 slit green chillies
- 1 tsp. red chilli powder
- ½ tsp. turmeric powder
- ½ tsp. garam masala powder
- 1 tsp. ginger-garlic paste
- 1 tbsp. lemon juice
- 1 tbsp. chopped mint leaves
- 1 tbsp. finely chopped fresh coriander leaves
- 1 small piece of cinnamon
- 2 cloves
- 1 bay leaf
- 2 green cardamom pods
- ¼ tsp. asafoetida
- ½ tsp. cumin seeds
- 3 tbsp. ghee
- Salt for seasoning

Bringing everything together

1. Season the riced cauliflower with salt and cook with one tbsp. of ghee on low heat until done and tender. You can sprinkle a little bit of water as needed. Once done, keep it aside.

2. In a thick-bottomed pan or kadhai on medium heat, melt the remaining ghee, add the cumin seeds and let them splutter. Then add the whole spices and fry for a few seconds.

3. Add the asafoetida and after a few seconds, add the sliced onions. Fry for a few minutes until they are almost golden, add the ginger-garlic paste and fry further for 2–3 minutes.

4. Add the tomatoes and cook until they soften.

5. Add the bell peppers and mushrooms and cook for a few minutes and afterwards, put in the fried paneer.

6. Add the spice powders: turmeric, red chilli powder, garam masala, mint leaves and a little salt. The cauliflower rice is already seasoned so you can always adjust the seasoning accordingly once everything is mixed in.

7. Gently mix in the cooked cauliflower rice and mix everything well together, add the lemon juice, cover the pan with a lid and let it cook for 3–4 minutes.

8. Add the fresh coriander and let it cook for a minute or so. Serve it with raita made with seasoned Greek yoghurt and sliced onions.

Tip: If you want to add greens like methi or spinach, add them at the same time as the bell peppers and mushrooms.

Nutritional Information Per Serving

Serving Size – 2

Amount Per Serving

Calories 332

Total Fat 28 g

Total Carbohydrate 10 g

Protein 7 g

Thalipeeth

This Maharashtrian household staple is a combination of several flours and while it's great to enjoy if you are not on Keto, it would be unfair to not be able to eat it while on the Keto diet. Hopefully, this version and some white butter will let some of us still enjoy it.

Ingredients

½ cup of chopped methi or fenugreek leaves
20 gms soya flour
30 gms almond flour
50 gms grated paneer
¼ cup finely chopped onions
½ tsp. finely grated ginger
1–2 finely chopped green chillies
½ tsp. turmeric powder
1 tsp. red chilli powder
1 tsp. coriander powder
½ tsp. garam masala
2 tsp. sesame seeds
¼ cup chopped fresh coriander leaves or cilantro
3 tbsp. ghee
Salt to taste
Warm water as needed to knead the dough
1 tbsp. white butter

Bringing everything together

1. In a mixing bowl, add the soya flour, almond flour, grated paneer, onions, ginger, green chillies and the spice powders: turmeric, chilli powder, garam masala and salt. Add the chopped methi and fresh coriander leaves along with a spoon of the ghee.

2. Using the warm water a little at a time, make a firm dough and let it rest for few minutes.

3. Divide the dough into similar sized balls and start heating a flat pan on medium heat.

4. Use either a sheet of foil or a baking sheet or parchment paper or even a Ziploc bag cut open, first grease it with a little bit of ghee to spread the thalipeeth dough. Take one dough ball and slowly spread it over the sheet. Make sure that it isn't too thin by patting the dough with gentle pressure using your fingers.

5. Once you have patted the dough into a disc shape, slowly lift the sheet and turn it over the pan. This way, the thalipeeth will transfer onto the pan.

6. Sprinkle some sesame seeds onto the thalipeeth and using a finger, make 3–4 indentations or holes on the surface.

7. Grease the sides and the top of the thalipeeth with ghee and let it cook.

8. After about 3–4 minutes using a flat spatula, slowly flip the thalipeeth over and spread some more ghee on it and let it cook till both sides are evenly cooked.

9. Use the remaining dough similarly.

10. Serve it with a dollop of white butter.

Tip: If you do not have methi on hand, use spinach or palak or moringa leaves or any other vegetable that is Keto friendly for your thalipeeth to increase the fibre intake.

Nutritional Information Per Serving
Serving Size – 2

Amount Per Serving
Calories 500
Total Fat 47 g
Total Carbohydrate 4 g
Protein 14 g

If you are thinking of starting the Keto diet, we would highly recommend starting with Intermittent Fasting and then getting on the Keto diet. Take the 7-day free challenge at https://www.ketomonk.com/bonus.

Paneer Tikka Wraps

This recipe uses lettuce leaves for wrapping the tikka, but you can marinate a batch of paneer and use it either as a snack or use a parantha to make a wrap.

Ingredients

200 gms paneer, cut into cubes
1 cup fresh coriander leaves
¼ cup fresh mint leaves
2 green chillies (according to taste)
1 tsp ginger-garlic paste
½ tsp. garam masala powder
½ tsp. chaat masala
1 tsp. lemon juice
1 tbsp. full-fat yoghurt
A few onion rings sprinkled with lemon juice and chaat masala for garnish
3 tbsp. ghee
5–6 leaves of either romaine or iceberg lettuce
Salt for seasoning

Bringing everything together

1. In a blender, add the fresh coriander and mint leaves, green chillies, ginger-garlic paste with yoghurt and make a paste.

2. Put the paneer cubes into a bowl and add the green paste, the spice powders: garam masala and chaat masala, lemon juice and salt for seasoning.

3. Coat the paneer cubes with everything and let it marinate for 30 minutes to an hour. You can always freeze marinated paneer or refrigerate it to use at a later time.

4. In a pan, melt the ghee and fry the paneer cubes until brown, crispy and done.

5. Wash the lettuce and dry it. Spoon a few cubes of the
    paneer tikka into the leaves and garnish with the onion
    rings sprinkled with lemon juice and chaat masala.

Tip: You can add onions, bell peppers or mushrooms to the marinade
too and cook it with the paneer.

Nutritional Information Per Serving
Serving Size – 2

Amount Per Serving
Calories 523
Total Fat 46 g
Total Carbohydrate 13 g
Protein 18 g

Paneer Sandwich

This sandwich can be prepped for in advance and can be made quickly once you have everything ready and chopped up.

Ingredients

200 gms paneer

2 tbsp. butter

1 small bunch of fresh coriander leaves

½ cup fresh mint leaves

1 tsp. chopped ginger

2 green chillies (according to taste)

1 tsp. lemon juice

½ tsp. amchoor (hereafter referred to as dried mango powder)

½ tsp. chaat masala

2 tsp. cream cheese

50 gms thinly sliced onions

50 gms thinly sliced bell peppers or capsicum

30 gms thinly sliced tomatoes

50 gms thinly sliced cucumbers

Salt and pepper for seasoning

Bringing everything together

1. Prepare the green chutney for the sandwich first. Clean and wash the fresh coriander and mint leaves.

2. In a blender, add the fresh coriander and mint leaves, chopped ginger, green chillies, lemon juice and dried mango powder. Blend this well using very little water and season with salt. (Note: The lemon juice and dried mango powder will make it slightly salty and tangy.)

3. Slice the paneer into thick slices. 200 gms of paneer should easily yield about four slices.

4. In a pan, on low to medium heat, melt the butter and fry the paneer slices till they are brown and crispy on both sides.

5. Place two paneer pieces flat on a plate or tray, spread some green chutney, cream cheese and place a few slices each of onions, bell peppers, tomatoes and cucumbers. Sprinkle salt, pepper and chaat masala.

6. Place the remaining two paneer slices on top of the first two to resemble a sandwich and enjoy.

Tip: You can add other vegetables as well. I sometimes add some extra cheese to the sandwich and cook the sandwich again in the pan for a couple of minutes to melt it slightly.

Nutritional Information Per Serving
Serving Size – 2

Amount Per Serving
Calories 503
Total Fat 42 g
Total Carbohydrate 6 g
Protein 23 g

Lemon Rice

Lemon rice is a great dish for times when you need to make something quickly—either after a busy day or when you are in a rush in the morning and need to make lunch.

Ingredients

2 cups riced cauliflower
3–4 slit green chillies
1 tbsp. peanuts
1 sprig of curry leaves
1 tsp. mustard seeds
1 tbsp. finely chopped coriander leaves
2 dried red chillies
¼ tsp. asafoetida
1 tsp. turmeric powder
½ cup lemon juice
2 ½ tbsp. ghee
Salt to taste

Bringing everything together

1. Season the riced cauliflower with salt and cook with one tbsp. of ghee on low heat until tender and cooked. You can sprinkle some water as needed.

2. Transfer to a bowl and let it cool a little.

3. In a pan, heat up the remaining ghee on low heat till it melts. Increase the heat a little and add the mustard seeds. Once they start spluttering, add the green and red chillies and fry for a minute. Add the asafoetida and curry leaves and fry for a few more seconds.

4. Add the peanuts and let them fry for a minute or more till they turn slightly darker and lastly, add the turmeric and mix everything well.

5. Switch off the heat and let it cool for a few minutes. Pour in the lemon juice.

6. Add the cooked riced cauliflower to the pan and mix everything well. Taste and add more salt or lemon juice if you think it's not sour enough. Top it up with finely chopped, fresh coriander leaves.

Nutritional Information Per Serving
Serving Size – 2

Amount Per Serving
Calories 243
Total Fat 22 g
Total Carbohydrate 8 g
Protein 4 g

Avial

Avial is one of my childhood favourites and for those of you who enjoy it, it can be a Keto friendly dish as well. It traditionally uses root vegetables but since not all of them can be consumed on Keto, we can add the ones that are allowed.

Ingredients

1 cup fresh grated coconut
1 tsp. cumin seeds
2–3 green chillies (according to taste)
¼ cup full-fat yoghurt
2 tsp. coconut oil
¼ tsp. asafoetida
A sprig of curry leaves
1 tsp. mustard seeds
2 long dried red chillies
½ cup ash gourd (white pumkin) pieces
¼ cup beans, cut lengthwise
1 small brinjal, cut into big cubes
1 tsp. turmeric powder
Salt for seasoning

Bringing everything together

1. In a blender, blend the coconut, cumin seeds and green chillies with a splash of water.

2. In a saucepan, boil the vegetables along with the turmeric and salt in about 1.5 to 2 cups of water. Make sure that the vegetables don't turn too mushy.

3. Once done, add the coconut paste and blend everything well together, seasoning further with salt if needed.

4. Let this come to a boil which may take a few minutes. Once it boils for about 2–3 minutes, turn off the heat.

5. Add the yoghurt and blend everything well. (You can skip the yoghurt as it's optional.)

6. In a small seasoning or sauté pan, heat up the coconut oil and add the mustard seeds. Once they splutter, add the dried red chillies, curry leaves and asafoetida. Add the seasoning to the avial and serve.

Tip: Use as many or as little vegetables as your macros will allow you. You can add zucchini or chayote squash if that is what you have on hand.

Nutritional Information Per Serving
Serving Size – 2

Amount Per Serving
Calories 213
Total Fat 19 g
Total Carbohydrate 9 g
Protein 3 g

Paneer Paniyaram

Paniyaram is eaten for breakfast or as an evening snack. It is quite easy to put together. Paniyarams are made in a special pan which has in-built circular depressions. These pans are widely and easily available.

Ingredients

200 gms. paneer or cottage cheese

3 tbsp. ghee or coconut oil for greasing

½ cup of finely chopped onions

2 finely chopped green chillies

1 tsp. mustard seeds

8–10 curry leaves

¼ cup finely chopped fresh coriander leaves

2 tsp. finely chopped ginger

¼ tsp. asafoetida

Salt to taste

Bringing it together

1. Grate the paneer, blend in a blender until it is fine and transfer to a bowl.

2. In a small pan, warm up about a tbsp. of ghee or oil and when its heated up, add the mustard seeds and let them splutter. Add asafoetida, green chillies and curry leaves and fry for a minute.

3. Add the onion and sauté for a couple of minutes and then add the ginger and fry until the onions are translucent.

4. Turn off the heat and let this mixture cool for a few minutes. Add this to the bowl with the paneer along with the fresh coriander and season with salt.

5. Blend everything well and using the palms of your hands make little balls of the paneer.

6. Heat the paniyaram pan and add a few drops of ghee in each mould. Place a paneer ball in each and grease generously with ghee or oil.

7. Cook until the side facing the pan is almost brown and then gently flip and cook until the entire paniyaram is evenly cooked and browned.

8. Serve with a chutney of your choice.

Tip: You can add some Keto friendly vegetables like finely chopped green beans or bell peppers to increase the fiber content.

Nutritional Information Per Serving

Serving Size – 2

Amount Per Serving

Calories 343

Total Fat 28 g

Total Carbohydrate 3 g

Protein 18 g

Keto Thayir Sadam

My husband and I enjoy a little bit of Thayir Sadam or seasoned curd rice every now and then. This is a quick recipe if you have riced cauliflower on hand.

Ingredients

2 cups riced cauliflower
1.5 cups full-fat Greek yoghurt or hung curd
1 tsp. grated ginger
½ tsp. mustard seeds
¼ tsp. asafoetida
1 tbsp. finely chopped fresh coriander leaves
1 sprig of curry leaves
3–4 dried button red chillies or 2 long dried red chillies
2 tbsp. ghee
Salt to taste

Bringing everything together

1. Season the riced cauliflower with salt and cook with one tbsp. of ghee on low heat until tender. You can sprinkle a little bit of water as needed to cook the riced cauliflower.

2. Transfer to a bowl and let it cool a little. Add the grated ginger, yoghurt or hung curd and fresh coriander leaves and mix well. Season with salt as needed, since the riced cauliflower has been seasoned while cooking too. Adjust the amount of curd depending on how you like the consistency of the curd rice.

3. In a seasoning pan or a small sauté pan, heat up the remaining ghee on low heat till it melts. Add the mustard seeds and as they start spluttering, add the red chillies and let them fry for a couple of minutes until they turn slightly

dark. Add the asafoetida and curry leaves and fry for a few seconds.

4. Add this seasoning to the curd rice and mix everything well.

Nutritional Information Per Serving
Serving Size – 2

Amount Per Serving
Calories 327
Total Fat 24 g
Total Carbohydrate 10 g
Protein 17 g

Paneer Pakodas

The rainy days are perfect for chai and pakodas. Try the paneer pakoda recipe whenever you want to enjoy this favourite desi snack.

Ingredients

100 gms paneer (cut lengthwise like thick fries)

2 tbsp. almond flour

½ tsp. turmeric powder

2 tsp. red chilli powder

½ tsp. garam masala

Pinch of asafoetida

½ tsp. chaat masala

Salt to taste

2 tbsp. ghee for shallow frying

Bringing everything together

1. Soak the paneer pieces in warm water for about ten minutes to soften them.

2. In a bowl, mix the almond flour, turmeric and red chilli powder, salt, asafoetida and garam masala.

3. Drain the paneer pieces, leave a little moisture on them and coat them with the flour and spice mix and ensure that they are well coated.

4. In a shallow pan, heat the ghee and slowly, put the paneer pieces into the pan. Fry on all sides till crispy and done. Sprinkle with chaat masala.

5. Serve with either green mint chutney or a dip of your choice.

Tip: If Halloumi cheese is easily available, you can substitute the paneer with it and try halloumi pakodas. You can use the spice mix for other pakodas too using vegetables like cauliflower, brinjal, zucchini or even lauki.

Nutritional Information Per Serving
Serving Size – 2

Amount Per Serving
Calories 354
Total Fat 33 g
Total Carbohydrate 1 g
Protein 12 g

Paneer and Capsicum Rings

This dish can be eaten as a heavy snack or a meal if accompanied by a salad or a smoothie. You can make extra filling and re-use it for another meal or use it in a parantha.

Ingredients

2 medium sized bell peppers or capsicum
150 gms paneer
1 tsp. finely chopped green chillies
¼ tsp. finely grated ginger
1 tsp. red chilli powder
½ tsp. garam masala
1 tsp. chaat masala
1 tbsp. finely chopped fresh coriander leaves
2 tsp. lemon juice
2 tbsp. ghee for greasing and cooking
Salt for seasoning

Bringing it together

1. Cut the top and bottom of the bell peppers, deseed and remove the core so that each piece is hollow. Cut them into rings which are half-inch thick. This should yield about eight rings or so.

2. Crumble the paneer into tiny pieces or grate it. In a bowl, add the paneer, spice powders, fresh coriander leaves and lemon juice and season with salt.

3. In a plate or on the chopping board, place the capsicum rings flat and pack them tightly with the paneer filling.

4. Take a flat-bottomed pan, the bigger the better since you can get more rings in at a time. Heat up the pan and add some ghee to it and once slightly hot, slowly transfer the

rings one at a time to the pan. Make sure that you don't overlap them.

5. Drizzle some ghee on top of the rings, cover with a lid and cook for a couple of minutes on medium heat.

6. Flip the rings carefully with a wide spatula, cover and cook again for a couple of minutes till you feel that the bell pepper rings have softened.

7. Uncover and again cook both sides for a couple of minutes each until they are nicely brown and done.

8. Serve with a simple dip made from Greek yoghurt mixed with red chilli powder, salt and chaat masala.

Tip: You can add vegetables like bell peppers, mushrooms and broccoli to the paneer stuffing as well. Cut them up into small pieces, season, and cook for a few minutes before adding them to the paneer stuffing.

Nutritional Information Per Serving
Serving Size – 2

Amount Per Serving
Calories 433
Total Fat 37 g
Total Carbohydrate 7 g
Protein 17 g

Mushroom Masala

Mushrooms are very versatile and can be cooked in different ways. I sometimes keep it simple by pairing them in a stir-fry with spinach, in a pulao or mix them with other vegetables in a curry. This recipe is a good side dish to serve with roti or parantha.

Ingredients

200 gms sliced mushrooms
½ cup sliced onions
¼ cup chopped tomatoes
2 slit green chillies
½ tsp. red chilli powder
¼ tsp. turmeric powder
½ tsp. garam masala powder
1 tsp. ginger-garlic paste
1 tsp. lemon juice
1 tbsp. finely chopped fresh coriander leaves
½ tsp. fennel or saunf seeds
3 tbsp. ghee
Salt for seasoning

Bringing everything together

1. In a pan, heat up the ghee and once it melts, add the fennel or saunf seeds and let them splutter.

2. Add the sliced onions and let them fry until they turn golden.

3. Add the ginger-garlic paste and fry for 3–4 minutes and put the chopped tomatoes in.

4. Cook them until they soften, add the chilli powder, turmeric powder and garam masala and cook for a couple of minutes.

5. Add the sliced mushrooms and sauté. The mushrooms will release water and cook in a few minutes. Keep sauteing until the mushrooms dry up.

6. Add lemon juice, mix everything well and garnish with fresh coriander leaves.

Tip: If you want to add greens like methi or spinach, add them a few minutes after the mushrooms. You can add bell peppers too.

Nutritional Information Per Serving
Serving Size – 2

Amount Per Serving
Calories 256
Total Fat 23 g
Total Carbohydrate 8 g
Protein 4 g

Kadhi

Kadhi is comfort food for a lot of us and you can enjoy it while on the Keto diet with this version.

Ingredients

1 cup full-fat Greek yoghurt or full-fat hung curd
2 tbsp. sour cream
1 tbsp. almond flour
1 tsp. ginger-green chilli paste
1 small piece of cinnamon
2 cloves
½ tsp asafoetida
½ tsp. cumin seeds
6–7 curry leaves
2 tbsp. ghee
1 tbsp. finely chopped fresh coriander leaves
Salt for seasoning
Pinch of sweetener (if needed)

Bringing everything together

1. In a small bowl, combine the sour cream and almond flour and whisk it until blended.

2. In a thick-bottomed pan or kadhai on medium heat, melt the ghee and add the cumin seeds and let them splutter. Add the curry leaves, cinnamon, cloves and let them fry for a few seconds and then add the asafoetida.

3. Turn down the heat, add the sour cream and almond flour mixture along with the Greek yoghurt and some water and whisk everything until blended.

4. Add the ginger-green chilli paste and keep stirring the mixture on low heat till it is all blended together.

5. Increase the heat slightly to let the kadhi come to a gentle boil. It will become thicker. Be careful that the curd doesn't split.

6. Season with salt and add a pinch of sweetener if you like your kadhi to be a little sweet (like I do).

7. Add the fresh coriander and let it cook for a minute or so. Serve it with either some cauliflower jeera rice or pulao.

Tip: Like the roasted powders, you can always keep some ginger and green chilli paste on hand and store it in a refrigerator or freezer. Crush some ginger and green chillies with a little salt in a mortar and pestle or grind them in a blender. You can use the paste for paranthas or other vegetable dishes as well.

Nutritional Information Per Serving
Serving Size – 3

Amount Per Serving
Calories 233
Total Fat 21 g
Total Carbohydrate 5 g
Protein 7 g

Kick-start your weight loss journey by joining our 7-day challenge at https://www.ketomonk.com/bonus.

Soya Nuggets Sabzi

A lot of people are still divided about soya nuggets and would not recommend it for a Ketogenic diet but sometimes, these offer a good change especially for vegetarians. Make these once in a while and make sure you track your macros.

Ingredients

2 cups of soya nuggets (I prefer the smaller size)

½ cup finely chopped onions

½ cup finely chopped tomatoes

2 sliced green chillies (according to taste)

½ tsp. finely chopped ginger

½ tsp. finely chopped garlic

1 tsp. garam masala powder

½ tsp. red chilli powder

½ tsp. turmeric powder

2 tbsp. ghee

1 small piece of cinnamon

2 cloves

¼ tsp. full-fat cream

2 tbsp. finely chopped fresh coriander leaves

Salt for seasoning

Bringing everything together

1. Put the soya nuggets into a bowl and cover them with hot water—maybe three cups or so and let them stand for 20–30 minutes. Squeeze out the water and keep them aside.

2. In a pan, on medium heat, melt the ghee and add the cinnamon, cloves and green chillies and fry for a minute. Add the onions and let them fry for 3–4 minutes.

3. Add the ginger and garlic and fry until the onions are browned. Add the chopped tomatoes and let them cook until they soften.

4. Add the spices: red chilli, turmeric and garam masala and blend them in.

5. Next, add the drained soya nuggets and blend them well with the masala. Season with salt and add half cup of water. Cover with a lid and let it cook for about ten minutes or so, taking care that you stir it a couple of times in between.

6. Uncover the pan and cook for an extra 3–4 minutes, making sure that most of the water evaporates. Add the cream and mix well and cook for one more minute or so.

7. Garnish with fresh coriander.

Tip: If you have mushrooms or bell peppers on hand, you can add them to this as well. I particularly love mushrooms with soya nuggets.

Nutritional Information Per Serving
Serving Size – 2

Amount Per Serving
Calories 346
Total Fat 28 g
Total Carbohydrate 13 g
Protein 10 g

Sarson Ka Saag

This winter favourite takes some effort but is totally worth it. You can always make extra and freeze or refrigerate to relish it again.

Ingredients

1 bunch of mustard/sarson leaves

½ bunch of spinach leaves

½ bunch of bathua/chaakvat/cheel/chenopodium/paruppu keerai leaves

3 sliced green chillies (according to taste)

2 tsp. finely chopped ginger

3 tsp. finely chopped garlic

1 cup finely chopped onions (reserve one teaspoon for tempering)

1 cup finely chopped tomatoes

½ tsp. red chilli powder

1 tsp. coriander powder

3 tbsp. ghee

1 tbsp. almond flour

1 tsp. lemon juice

1 tbsp. fresh cream

Salt for seasoning

Bringing everything together

1. First step would be to prep all the greens. For the mustard greens, remove thick stems if any and retain the leaves. Clean the other two bunches of greens as well. You can also add radish greens.

2. Wash the greens several times to remove any soil or dirt. Once cleaned, chop them and put them into a pressure cooker or a wide pan.

3. Add the chopped onions, tomatoes, green chillies, ginger and garlic. Add a cup of water and pressure cook the greens for about 5–6 whistles.

4. If you are making this in a pan, add enough water and let it cook.

5. Once cool, transfer the mixture into a blender or a food processor or use a hand blender to blend everything well. If you like some texture to your saag, you can keep it a little coarse.

6. In a pan, melt a tbsp. of the ghee, add the pureed mixture, season with salt and add the red chilli powder and the coriander powder.

7. Mix a little water with the almond flour and add this to the mixture. Let this come to a gentle boil on medium heat (make sure to keep stirring the mixture).

8. While this is almost done, in a small sauté pan, melt the remaining ghee and add the reserved teaspoon of onions. Fry until they turn golden and pour this tempering over the saag mixture.

9. Garnish with fresh cream and serve it with a parantha or roti of your choice.

Tip: You can add a few pieces of chopped white radish while cooking the greens, this is a nice addition.

Nutritional Information Per Serving
Serving Size – 3

Amount Per Serving
Calories 281
Total Fat 24 g
Total Carbohydrate 9 g
Protein 5 g

Coconut Dosa

A lot of us miss dosas on Keto so this simple recipe should help on days when you want to have them. Serve it up with chutney or spike the batter with green chillies, onions, chopped fresh coriander and curry leaves.

Ingredients

2 tbsp. coconut flour
3 tbsp. coconut milk
1 tbsp. fresh grated coconut
1 tbsp. ghee
¼ tsp. salt

Bringing everything together

1. In a blender, add the coconut flour, coconut milk and fresh grated coconut and grind into a fine paste. Season with salt.

2. Add a little more coconut milk in case the batter seems too thick. You need consistency in the batter that can be easily poured and spread on a pan.

3. Put a pan on heat and melt some ghee. Using a ladle, pour some of the batter on the pan and spread it evenly on it.

4. Let it cook for a couple of minutes till the edges start getting crisp and the bottom of the dosa becomes a little brown. Slowly, loosen the dosa from the pan using a spatula and flip it. Cook for another couple of minutes until both sides are done and serve.

Nutritional Information Per Serving

Serving Size – 1

Amount Per Serving

Calories 221

Total Fat 20 g

Total Carbohydrate 3 g

Protein 2 g

Malai Paneer Bhurji

This one is a Keto favourite. There are many variations of this recipe so do give this creamy treat a shot.

Ingredients

200 gms paneer
½ cup finely chopped onions
½ cup finely chopped tomatoes
½ cup bell peppers or capsicum
1–2 finely chopped green chillies
1 tsp. finely grated ginger
1 tsp. finely minced garlic
½ tsp. cumin seeds
1 tsp. red chilli powder
½ tsp. turmeric powder
1 tsp. Kasuri methi
1 tsp. garam masala
1 tbsp. heavy cream
2 tbsp. ghee
1 tbsp. finely chopped fresh coriander leaves
Salt to taste

Bringing everything together

1. Cut the paneer into big chunks and soak them in warm water for about 15–20 minutes to soften.
2. Grate the paneer into small pieces or crumble them finely. The key is to have crumbled paneer without any lumps.
3. In a pan, melt the ghee and splutter the cumin seeds.
4. Add the green chillies and fry for a few seconds. Next, add the onions and sauté for a couple of minutes.

5. Add the ginger and garlic and fry with the onions until they turn slightly golden.

6. Add the tomatoes and cook until they soften and you see the ghee leaving the sides of the pan.

7. Add the red chilli powder, turmeric powder, garam masala and Kasuri methi and fry for a couple of minutes. Add the chopped bell peppers and sauté for 2–3 minutes.

8. Add the grated paneer, season with salt and blend the paneer into the masala. Add a little water and cover the pan.

9. Let it cook for about 7–8 minutes and check in between to make sure that it doesn't stick to the pan.

10. Lower the heat, add the cream and slowly blend everything together once more and cook for a few more minutes.

11. Garnish with finely chopped fresh coriander and serve.

Nutritional Information Per Serving
Serving Size – 3

Amount Per Serving
Calories 374
Total Fat 31 g
Total Carbohydrate 6 g
Protein 16 g

Cauliflower Thengai Sadam
(Cauliflower Coconut Rice)

If you have riced cauliflower and fresh grated coconut on hand, this dish comes together in a matter of minutes. Serve it with avial or keerai masiyal or coconut chutney and enjoy.

Ingredients

2 cups riced cauliflower

2–3 green chillies (sliced lengthwise)

½ tsp. cumin seeds

½ tsp. mustard seeds

2 tbsp. fresh grated coconut

1 tsp. finely grated ginger

¼ tsp. asafoetida

8–10 fresh curry leaves

2 tsp. peanuts

2 tbsp. ghee or coconut oil

1 tbsp. finely chopped coriander leaves

Salt to season

Bringing everything together

1. Season the riced cauliflower with salt and cook with one tbsp. of ghee on low heat until done and tender. You can sprinkle a little bit of water as needed.

2. Transfer it to a bowl and let it cool a little.

3. In another pan, melt the remaining ghee or coconut oil and splutter the cumin and mustard seeds and once done, add the peanuts, green chillies, asafoetida and fry for a couple of minutes.

4. Add the ginger and curry leaves and sauté for a minute.

5. Add the fresh grated coconut and fry for 3–4 minutes, you do not need to brown the coconut.

6. Add the cooked riced cauliflower, fresh coriander leaves and season with salt. Mix everything thoroughly and cook for another couple of minutes. Serve hot with either chutney or sambar or avial.

Nutritional Information Per Serving
Serving Size – 2

Amount Per Serving
Calories 203
Total Fat 19 g
Total Carbohydrate 3 g
Protein 3 g

If you are on Keto diet, take your weight loss journey to the next level with Intermittent Fasting. We have a 7-day challenge that you can sign up for FREE at https://www.ketomonk.com/bonus.

Spinach and Cheese Grilled Sandwich

This sandwich is similar to the paneer sandwich but uses a filling of spinach (palak) and cheese. As with the other sandwich, you can always make extra filling in advance and use it as and when needed.

Ingredients

200 gms paneer
2 cups chopped spinach
3 tbsp. butter
¼ cup finely chopped onions
1 finely minced garlic pod
¼ cup green or coloured bell peppers (diced into small pieces)
1 finely chopped green chilli
¼ cup cream
½ cup shredded cheese (use what you have on hand, mozzarella or cheddar)
½ tsp. chaat masala or Italian seasoning (depending on your preference)
Salt and pepper to season

Bringing everything together

1. Slice the paneer into thick slices. 200 gms of paneer should easily yield about four slices.

2. In a pan, melt about ½ tbsp of butter and sauté the onions and garlic until the onions turn translucent.

3. Add the finely chopped green chilli, diced bell peppers and fry for a minute.

4. Add the chopped spinach and cook for a few minutes until it wilts.

5. Add the cream and ¼ cup of the shredded cheese and blend everything well.

6. Season with salt, pepper and either chaat masala or Italian seasoning.

7. Cook until the cream is incorporated and the cheese has slightly melted.

8. Take the pan off the heat and keep aside.

9. In another pan on low to medium heat, melt the remaining butter and fry the paneer slices till they are brown and crispy on both sides.

10. First place two paneer pieces flat on the pan. Divide the cheese and spinach mixture into two portions and spread one portion on each of the paneer pieces. Add the remaining ¼ cup of shredded cheese.

11. Place the remaining two paneer slices on top of the first two to resemble a sandwich and cook for about a minute on each side until the cheese melts completely. Serve with a dip of your choice.

Nutritional Information Per Serving
Serving Size – 2

Amount Per Serving
Calories 771
Total Fat 68 g
Total Carbohydrate 6 g
Protein 30 g

Soya Pudina Pulao

This riced cauliflower dish with soya nuggets and mint involves some prepping but you can multitask some steps and get it ready in a jiffy as well.

Ingredients

2 cups riced cauliflower
1½ cups of chopped fresh mint leaves
¼ cup fresh grated coconut
1 cup paneer cubes
½ cup of chopped fresh coriander leaves
2–3 green chillies (according to taste)
2 tsp. ginger-garlic paste (you can always substitute this with fresh and finely chopped ginger and garlic if you do not have the paste on hand)
½ tsp. cumin seeds
¼ cup finely chopped onions
1 small stick of cinnamon
2 bay leaves
1 pod of green cardamom
¼ tsp. asafoetida
1 cup soya nuggets (preferably the smaller sized ones)
4 tbsp. ghee
1 tbsp. finely chopped coriander leaves
Salt to season

Bringing everything together

1. First, soak the soya nuggets in a bowl with hot water and salt for half an hour.

2. Season the riced cauliflower with salt and cook with one tbsp. of ghee on low heat until done and tender. You can sprinkle a little bit of water as needed.

3. Transfer the cooked riced cauliflower to a bowl and let it cool a little.

4. In a blender, adding very little water, make a fine paste of fresh mint and coriander leaves, fresh grated coconut, green chillies and ginger-garlic paste.

5. In a small pan, add one tbsp. of ghee and lightly fry the paneer cubes until they are slightly brown.

6. Prepping the soya nuggets, riced cauliflower and the mint paste in tandem will let you get started with putting the pulao together.

7. In a wide and heavy pan on medium heat, first melt the ghee.

8. Add the cumin seeds, cinnamon stick, bay leaves and the cardamom pod and fry for a minute.

9. Add the chopped onions and sauté till they turn translucent and add the mint paste.

10. Cook the mint paste until you can no longer smell the rawness of the ginger and garlic and the ghee starts leaving the sides of the paste. This will easily take about 6–7 minutes.

11. Drain and squeeze all the water out of the soya nuggets and add them to the pan. Cook for a couple of minutes.

12. Next, add the cooked riced cauliflower and gently mix it with the mint paste and the soya nuggets until everything is blended well together.

13. Season with salt and sprinkle a few drops of water. Cover the pan with a lid and let it cook further for about 3–4 minutes.

14. Garnish with finely chopped fresh coriander and fried paneer cubes and turn off the heat. Serve it hot with a raita of your choice.

Tip: You can add vegetables like mushrooms, bell peppers or whatever you have on hand if it fits into your macros.

Nutritional Information Per Serving
Serving Size – 2

Amount Per Serving
Calories 538
Total Fat 48 g
Total Carbohydrate 11 g
Protein 14 g

Cucumber Dosa

Cucumber dosas need no fermentation and can be made with a few ingredients. You can whip up the batter just before a meal and enjoy them with a chutney or sambar of your choice.

Ingredients

    1 cup fresh grated coconut
    ½ cup coconut flour
    2–3 small sized cucumbers (look for tender ones with fewer and smaller seeds)
    ¼ cup unsweetened coconut water
    1 tsp. cumin seeds
    2 green chillies (according to taste)
    2 tbsp. ghee
    Salt to season

Bringing everything together

1. In a blender, blend together the fresh grated coconut, coconut flour, coconut water and green chillies and transfer to a bowl.

2. Peel and deseed the cucumbers and grate them.

3. Squeeze out some moisture from the cucumbers and transfer them to the bowl with the batter and season with salt.

4. Add the cumin seeds and mix everything well together. The consistency should be similar to any other dosa batter. Add water in case you need the batter to be a little thinner.

5. Heat up a griddle or pan or tava and grease it with a little ghee.

6. Using a ladle, pour some of the cucumber dosa batter on the pan and spread it with the back of the ladle to make a dosa.

7. Pour some ghee on the sides and let it cook.

8. Once you see the sides lifting up and the dosa becomes a little crispy and brown, gently flip it and cook for another minute.

9. Similarly, make dosas with the remaining batter.

Tip: I sometimes top the cucumber dosa with chopped onions, curry leaves, green chillies and finely chopped coriander to resemble uttapams. You can always use it as a base to add vegetables or ingredients of your choice.

Nutritional Information Per Serving
Serving Size – 2

Amount Per Serving
Calories 340
Total Fat 27 g
Total Carbohydrate 1 g
Protein 5 g

Sambar

Sambar or kuzhambhu (as known in Tamil Nadu) is traditionally made with toor dal (lentil) and tamarind. This recipe tries to replicate those flavours and this sambar can be eaten with coconut rice or dosa. You can use lauki or bottle gourd, yellow pumpkin, white pumpkin or ash gourd to give the sambar a slightly thicker consistency to replace the dal. You can add vegetables of your choice like brinjal, green beans or radish. Sambar powder uses lentils so in this recipe we'll skip that as well. The sourness of tamarind is replaced by adding lemon juice.

Ingredients

- 200 grams lauki or bottle gourd (chopped into cubes)
- 100 gms brinjal or eggplant (cut into cubes)
- ½ cup thinly sliced onions
- ½ cup finely chopped tomatoes
- 2–3 chopped green chillies (according to taste)
- 1 tsp. red chilli powder
- 2 ½ tsp. coriander powder
- 1 tsp. cumin powder
- 1 tsp. mustard seeds
- ¼ tsp. fenugreek seeds
- 10–12 curry leaves
- 2 dried red chillies
- ½ tsp. asafoetida
- 2 tbsp. ghee
- 1 tbsp. lemon juice
- 2 tbsp. finely chopped fresh coriander leaves
- Salt to season

Bringing everything together

1. In a pressure cooker, melt about ½ tbsp ghee and add ¼ cup of onions and sauté for a couple of minutes.

2. Add ¼ cup tomatoes and cook for another minute and add the chopped bottle gourd or lauki.

3. Add a cup of water and then add the coriander, cumin and red chilli powders along with the green chillies.

4. Season with a little salt and pressure cook for about 4–5 whistles so that the bottle gourd is cooked. Alternatively, you can cook this in a pan till the bottle gourd softens and can be mashed easily.

5. Once the bottle gourd is cooked, using the back of a ladle or a potato masher, gently mash the bottle gourd and put the cooker or pan again on low heat.

6. Add a little water and let it simmer.

7. In a different pan, melt the remaining ghee and splutter the mustard seeds.

8. When done, add the fenugreek seeds and cook for a minute.

9. Add the dried red chillies, asafoetida and the curry leaves and fry for a minute.

10. Add the remaining onions and tomatoes (1/4 cup of each) and cook for 4–5 minutes.

11. Add the brinjal pieces and fry for a couple more minutes and mix everything well.

12. Transfer this seasoning with the brinjal to the cooker or the pan and boil everything together until the brinjal is cooked well.

13. Add the fresh coriander and season with salt as needed.

14. Turn off the heat, add the lemon juice and mix everything once more.

15. You can add extra ghee to the sambar just before serving too.

Tip: You can replace the brinjal with greens like spinach or amaranth. You can also roast and add fresh grated coconut to the seasoning for a change in flavour.

Nutritional Information Per Serving
Serving Size – 2

Amount Per Serving
Calories 197
Total Fat 16 g
Total Carbohydrate 8 g
Protein 2 g

Kick-start your weight loss journey by joining our 7-day challenge at https://www.ketomonk.com/bonus.

Pumpkin Soup

As a child, I loved the tomato soup they served in restaurants with the croutons and would often have seconds! This pumpkin soup, similarly wholesome, is Keto friendly and can be made protein-rich by adding other vegetables like broccoli or spinach.

Ingredients

200 grams yellow pumpkin (cut into cubes)
½ tbsp. almond flour
2 tbsp. butter
2 tbsp. cream
1 bay leaf
1 tsp. finely minced garlic
¼ cup finely chopped onion
¼ tsp. of sweetener (optional)
Salt and ground pepper to season

Bringing everything together

1. Pressure cook the pumpkin with very little water for about 3–4 whistles. Alternatively, you can cook it in a saucepan with water until it softens but this will take longer.

2. In a pan, melt one tbsp. of butter, add the bay leaf and stir for a few seconds. Next, add the minced garlic and onion until the onion turns translucent.

3. Add the cooked pumpkin and mix it with the garlic and onion.

4. Let it cool down. Take out the bay leaf and reserve it. Using a hand blender or a food processor, puree the pumpkin mixture until smooth.

5. Put the pan back on heat and melt the remaining one tbsp.

of butter, add the bay leaf back and pour the pumpkin puree into the pan.

6. Add the almond flour and let the soup come to a gentle boil. The almond flour will thicken the consistency. You can skip it as well.

7. Season with salt, pepper and sweetener.

8. Adjust the consistency of the soup to your liking by adding water if needed. Stir in the cream and let it cook for another minute.

9. Serve hot with a side of vegetables or a salad.

Tip: You can add blanched broccoli or spinach while sautéing the pumpkin. You can also top it off with olive oil or more butter.

Nutritional Information Per Serving
Serving Size – 2

Amount Per Serving
Calories 204
Total Fat 18 g
Total Carbohydrate 9 g
Protein 2 g

Palak Paneer

Palak paneer is one of those ubiquitous Indian dishes that you find on menus everywhere from dhabas to restaurants and can be replicated in our homes very easily. Luckily for us, it's also one of those recipes that lends itself beautifully to be ketofied.

Ingredients

Making the puree

200 gms spinach (palak)
2 or more green chillies
3 cloves of garlic
½ inch of ginger
4 cups of water for blanching the spinach

Making the gravy

100 gms paneer cut into cubes
½ cup finely chopped onions
½ cup finely chopped tomato
2 cloves of garlic (finely chopped)
¼ tsp. asafoetida
½ tsp. cumin seeds
¼ tsp. turmeric powder
½ tsp. red chilli powder (if you feel that the green chillies will provide enough heat, skip this)
1 tsp. garam masala
1 bay leaf
2 tbsp. ghee or butter
½ tsp. Kasuri methi
1 tsp. lemon juice
Salt to taste
1 tsp. of cream and ginger juliennes (to garnish)

Bringing everything together

1. Clean the spinach leaves thoroughly by washing multiple times.

2. Boil four cups of water in a pan and once the water starts boiling, drop the spinach leaves into it and turn off the heat. Leave for a few minutes and strain the leaves. Do not discard the water and reserve for later.

3. Blend the blanched spinach, ginger, garlic and green chillies into a smooth paste and keep it aside.

4. Put a pan on heat and add the ghee or butter. Make sure to use lesser heat if you are using butter so that it doesn't burn. Once hot, add the asafoetida, cumin seeds and the bay leaf and let them crackle. Add the finely chopped onions and let them fry until they turn golden brown.

5. Add the finely chopped garlic and let it fry. Make sure it doesn't burn.

6. Add the finely chopped tomatoes and let them soften.

7. Once you see the fat releasing from the sides of the mixture, add the turmeric powder and chilli powders, Kasuri methi and garam masala. Fry for a minute.

8. Add the spinach puree and stir well. Add some of the reserved water and let it simmer for a few minutes till the spinach is cooked and all the masalas are incorporated well. Season with salt and add the lemon juice.

9. Add the cubed paneer and let it cook for a few minutes till the paneer softens.

10. Garnish with cream and ginger juliennes.

Nutritional Information Per Serving

Serving Size – 2

Amount Per Serving

Calories 362

Total Fat 28 g

Total Carbohydrate 9 g

Protein 15 g

Paneer Methi Cheese Marke Chilla

If you enjoy the desi version of pancakes then this recipe is perfect for you. Typically made with grains and flours, this one uses paneer and can be eaten for breakfast or a meal. You can also get innovative and add vegetables like zucchini or spinach (palak) or the greens from green onions. It's a good way to stick to your Keto diet and also get some fibre.

Ingredients

50 gms crumbled paneer (make sure there are no big lumps or pieces)

1 tsp. finely grated ginger

1 tsp. finely chopped green chillies

½ tsp. each of turmeric powder, chilli powder and garam masala

2 tbsp. chopped methi leaves

1 tbsp. finely chopped coriander leaves

2 tbsp. shredded cheese of your choice

1 tbsp. ghee or butter

2 tbsp. hung curd sprinkled with chaat masala for serving.

Bringing everything together

1.   In a bowl, combine all the ingredients except the ghee and make sure everything is well-blended.

2.   Heat up ghee in a pan and spread the mixture to make little pancakes or chillas.

3.   Cook till the chilla turns crisp and brown. Serve it with some hung curd sprinkled with chaat masala.

Nutritional Information Per Serving
Serving Size – 1

Amount Per Serving
Calories 372
Total Fat 33 g
Total Carbohydrate 4 g
Protein 13 g

Sausage Stir-fry

It is a good idea to have sausages handy on your Keto diet since they can be very useful when you are making a meal. You can eat them as is once they are cooked, add them to a frittata or an omelette or make a stir-fry. This recipe uses chicken sausages; you can replace them with ones you like. Also make sure that the sausages you buy are free of flours and fillers of any kind.

Ingredients

4 chicken sausages cut into big pieces (3–4 pieces from each sausage)

½ cup onions sliced lengthwise

½ cup coloured capsicums or peppers (sliced lengthwise)

¼ cup broccoli florets

½ cup mushrooms (cut into quarters)

2 tbsp. finely chopped garlic

2 tbsp. finely chopped ginger

1 tsp. finely chopped green chillies

1 tbsp. vinegar

1 tbsp. garam masala

2 tbsp. finely chopped coriander leaves

2 tbsp. butter

1 tbsp. olive oil

Salt and pepper to taste

Bringing everything together

1. In a pan, heat up olive oil and cook the chicken sausages till well done. Drain on a paper towel.

2. In the same pan, slowly melt the butter. Make sure you don't burn it. Add the green chillies, ginger and garlic and cook for a couple of minutes. Add the onions and cook till they are translucent.

3. Add the mushrooms and cook till they are done. Add the broccoli and capsicum and cook till they are tender and not mushy.

4. At this point, add the chicken sausage pieces back to the pan. Season with garam masala, salt, pepper and vinegar.

5. Mix everything well together and garnish with coriander leaves.

Nutritional Information Per Serving
Serving Size – 2

Amount Per Serving
Calories 381
Total Fat 20 g
Total Carbohydrate 11 g
Protein 22 g

Jhatpat Jhinga

If you are a prawn or shrimp fan, this recipe is for you. With ingredients that are found in most Indian homes and considering that one can cook prawns quickly, this can be made after a long day at work or to pack for lunch or when you need some comfort food.

Ingredients

100 gms prawns that have been shelled and deveined
¼ cup finely chopped onions
¼ cup finely chopped tomatoes
1 tsp. ginger-garlic paste
½ tsp. finely chopped green chillies
1 tbsp. finely chopped coriander leaves
1 tsp. red chilli powder
¼ tsp. turmeric powder
½ tsp. garam masala powder
1 tbsp. lemon juice
2 tbsp. oil
Salt to taste

Bringing everything together

1. In a pan, heat oil, add the onions and fry till they soften. Add the ginger-garlic paste and cook till the raw smell disappears and the onions have turned golden brown.

2. Add tomatoes and cook till they soften.

3. Add the red chilli and turmeric powder, garam masala and salt. Cook for a minute.

4. Add the prawns and cook till done. Make sure that you don't overcook the prawns as they will toughen up.

5. Add the lemon juice and mix well.

6. Garnish with coriander leaves.

Nutritional Information Per Serving

Serving Size – 1

Amount Per Serving

Calories 380

Total Fat 28 g

Total Carbohydrate 8 g

Protein 22 g

Desi Style Chicken and Broccoli Stir-fry

If you love Chinese food and think that you might have to miss it on your Keto diet, fret not. This recipe is tailor-made for the Chinese food lover!

Ingredients

200 gms boneless chicken (cut into small pieces)
50 gms broccoli (cut into florets)
1 tbsp. finely chopped ginger
1 tbsp. finely chopped garlic
3 stalks of spring onions (greens and whites separated and chopped)
1 ½ tbsp. chopped green chillies
2 tbsp. soya sauce
2 tbsp. red chilli sauce
2 tbsp. olive oil
½ tsp. sweetener
1 tbsp. butter
Salt and pepper to taste

Bringing everything together

1. In a pan on medium heat, melt the butter and add the chicken pieces. Season with salt and pepper and cook for fifteen minutes so that the chicken is cooked and browned. Keep aside.

2. In a wok or pan, heat up the olive oil and add the green chillies, garlic, ginger and the whites of the spring onions and cook for a few minutes.

3. Add the broccoli florets and sauté for a few minutes till they are tender but not mushy.

4. Add the sauces, sweetener and season further with salt and pepper as needed.

5. Mix the chicken into this and blend everything together. Cook for a few more minutes. Garnish with the greens from the spring onions.

Nutritional Information Per Serving

Serving Size – 2

Amount Per Serving

Calories 277

Total Fat 20 g

Total Carbohydrate 2 g

Protein 23 g

Keto Cauliflower Egg Fried Rice

Most of you have probably made excellent friends with cauliflower by now on your Keto diet and have used it as a replacement for rice. If you haven't done it so far, then use this recipe to get acquainted. Though this recipe uses eggs and a couple of vegetables, you can add chicken, bacon or shrimps as well.

Ingredients

1 small head of cauliflower (cut into florets)

2 eggs

2 stalks of spring onions (whites and greens separated)

1 tbsp. soya sauce

1 tbsp. green chilli paste

1 tbsp. finely chopped garlic

2 tbsp. ghee

1 tbsp. sesame oil

¼ cup thinly sliced beans

½ cup broccoli florets

Salt and pepper to taste

Bringing everything together

1. Clean the cauliflower and cut it into florets. Using a food processor or a mixer, grind it so that it has a rice like consistency. Make sure not to grind more than necessary or else the cauliflower will turn mushy.

2. Pour out the riced cauliflower onto a plate or tray lined with a paper towel or a muslin cloth. Squeeze and drain out as much moisture as possible.

3. Heat a pan with ghee, add the riced cauliflower and season it with salt and pepper. Let it cook for a few minutes. Take it out and keep aside.

Paneer and Capsicum Rings
(see, p. 47)

Coconut and Cream Barfi
(see, p. 161)

Strawberry
Smoothie and
Broccoli Paneer
Tikkis
(see, p. 119 and 137)

Kerala Style Egg Curry
and Methi Theplas
(see. p. 94 and 122)

Coconut Dosa and Coconut Chutney (see, p. 57 and 134)

Sausage Stir-fry
(see, p. 80)

Lauki ki Kheer (see, p. 147)

Paneer Sandwich (see, p. 35)

Pumpkin Soup (see, p. 73)

4. In the same pan, heat up the sesame oil and add garlic and whites of the spring onions and cook for two minutes.

5. Add the beans and cook till they are still crunchy. Add the broccoli at this stage and cook for 2–3 minutes.

6. Add the cauliflower rice back to the pan along with the soya sauce and green chilli sauce and season further as needed.

7. Beat the eggs and season with salt and pepper. Make a well in the cauliflower rice and pour the eggs in. Scramble the eggs and mix them into the rice as they cook.

8. Garnish with the greens of the spring onions and mix everything well before serving.

Nutritional Information Per Serving
Serving Size – 2

Amount Per Serving
Calories 347
Total Fat 27 g
Total Carbohydrate 11 g
Protein 11 g

Mast Masale Mussels

Mussels or clams are easily available in most markets. Once the initial cleaning is done, these don't take much time to cook and make up for the effort, thanks to their deliciousness.

Ingredients

250 gms mussels with their shells
½ cup finely chopped onions
¼ cup finely chopped tomatoes
2 tbsp. desiccated coconut
½ cup unsweetened coconut milk
2 tsp. red chilli powder
1 tsp. turmeric powder
2 tsp. garam masala
2 tsp. ginger-garlic paste
2 slit green chillies
2 tbsp. finely chopped coriander leaves
2 tbsp. coconut oil
Salt for seasoning

Bringing everything together

1. Clean the mussels in running water to make sure you remove all the sand and dirt.

2. Boil water in a pan and drop the mussels gently into the water. In a few minutes, the mussels will open. Turn off the heat and let them cool down. Discard the ones that haven't opened and gently wash the rest. You can either use both parts of the shell or use only the ones to which the flesh is attached.

3. In a wide-bottomed pan, heat the coconut oil, add the green chillies and let them splutter. Add the onions, ginger-garlic paste and fry till the onions are slightly

brown. Add the desiccated coconut and cook till it also turns slightly brown.

4. Add the tomatoes and cook them till they soften. Add the turmeric, chilli powders and garam masala and cook for a minute.

5. Drop the mussels slowly into the pan and gently coat the shells with the masala. Add salt to taste and let them cook for 5–6 minutes.

6. Add the coconut milk and let it simmer slowly for a few more minutes until done. Make sure it doesn't curdle.

7. Garnish with chopped coriander leaves.

Nutritional Information Per Serving
Serving Size – 2

Amount Per Serving
Calories 251
Total Fat 21 g
Total Carbohydrate 9 g
Protein 22 g

Saag Mutton

Saag Mutton is a delicate combination of spinach and mutton. You can serve it with Keto rotis or cauliflower jeera rice. Boneless mutton is preferred for this recipe. You can also substitute mutton with chicken.

Ingredients

200 gms boneless mutton
½ cup finely chopped onions
½ cup finely chopped tomatoes
1 cup pureed spinach
2 tbsp. ginger-garlic paste
1 tsp. of turmeric
1 tsp. red chilli powder
2 tsp. garam masala powder
2 slit green chillies
2 tbsp. ghee
1 tbsp. oil
1 small piece of cinnamon
1 bay leaf
1 tbsp. lemon juice
Salt to taste

Bringing everything together

1. In a pressure cooker, heat up the oil and add ghee to it. Add cinnamon, bay leaf and slit green chillies and fry for a minute.

2. Add the onions and fry till they soften and turn translucent. Add the ginger-garlic paste and cook for a couple of minutes. Add the mutton and cook on a high flame for a few minutes.

3. Add the chopped tomatoes and cook further till the tomatoes soften up. Add the turmeric, red chilli powder, salt and garam masala and cook for a minute.

4. Mix everything well and make sure the masala coats all the meat. Add a cup of water and cook for four whistles or till the mutton is tender and cooked.

5. Once the pressure is released, add the spinach puree and lemon juice. Cook for five minutes so that the puree blends well with the meat and the gravy.

Nutritional Information Per Serving
Serving Size – 2

Amount Per Serving
Calories 470
Total Fat 36 g
Total Carbohydrate 8 g
Protein 28 g

Tandoori Chicken Boti

An all-time favourite, tandoori chicken is a recipe most amateur cooks can master easily. It is preferable to use boneless chicken but you can also use the chicken pieces with bones. You can always marinate extra chicken and freeze it to use later.

Ingredients

200 gms boneless chicken pieces
2 tbsp. ghee
2 tbsp. ginger-garlic paste
3 tbsp. full-fat yoghurt
2 tsp. Kashmiri red chilli powder
1 tsp. garam masala
2 tbsp. lemon juice
2 tsp. tandoori masala
1 tsp. chaat masala
1 tbsp. oil
Salt to taste
Onion rings to serve

Bringing everything together

1. Wash and clean the chicken pieces.
2. In a bowl, make a marinade with ghee, ginger-garlic paste, yoghurt, red chilli powder, garam masala, tandoori masala and 1 tbsp. lemon juice. Add the chicken to it and make sure all the pieces are coated evenly.
3. Let it rest in the refrigerator for a couple of hours. If you are in a hurry, let it rest for half an hour.
4. Pre-heat the oven at 200 degrees Celsius. If you have skewers, skewer the chicken pieces and cook them in the oven for eight minutes. Brush the skewers with oil and cook for another 3–4 minutes until completely done.

5. If you don't have skewers, bake the chicken in a dish and turn the pieces half way through after brushing them with oil.

6. Once done, sprinkle chaat masala and the remaining lemon juice on the chicken and serve with onion rings.

Nutritional Information Per Serving
Serving Size – 2

Amount Per Serving
Calories 321
Total Fat 25 g
Total Carbohydrate 1 g
Protein 23 g

Get additional bonus material and access to a 7-day challenge by signing up at https://www.ketomonk.com/bonus.

Kerala Style Egg Curry

You can try this version of egg curry on days you'd like to have something different from the egg curry recipe you usually follow.

Ingredients

4 hard boiled eggs (cut into halves)
2 tbsp. coconut oil
½ cup finely chopped onions
½ cup finely chopped tomatoes
2 tsp. ginger-garlic paste
1 tsp. red chilli powder
½ tsp. black pepper
½ tsp. turmeric powder
1 tsp. garam masala
1 tsp. coriander powder
½ tsp. fennel (saunf) powder
½ cup unsweetened coconut milk
2 tbsp. chopped coriander leaves
5–6 curry leaves
2 slit green chillies
Salt to taste

Bringing everything together

1. In a pan, heat up the coconut oil, add the green chillies and let them splutter. Afterwards, add the curry leaves.

2. Add the onions and ginger-garlic paste. Sauté till the onions turn golden brown.

3. Now add the tomatoes and cook them till they soften.

4. Then add the dry masalas: red chilli powder, garam masala, coriander powder, turmeric powder and fennel powder. Cook for a couple of minutes.

5. Lower the flame and slowly add the coconut milk. Let it cook for a few minutes till the flavours blend together.

6. Place the eggs in the pan and spoon the curry over the eggs. Cover the pan and cook for 2–3 minutes. Add water to adjust the consistency of the curry.

7. Season with coriander leaves and serve.

Nutritional Information Per Serving
Serving Size – 2

Amount Per Serving
Calories 256
Total Fat 25 g
Total Carbohydrate 8g
Protein 14 g

Masala Fish Fry

Whenever you get bored of chicken or paneer, you can opt for this quick masala fish fry. It requires a short prep time. It is preferable to use fish like Basa, Surmai, Tilapia or Betki but you can easily use the locally available variety.

Ingredients

100 gms fish fillets

2 tsp. garlic paste

2 tsp. red chilli powder

1/2 tsp. turmeric powder

1 tbsp. finely chopped coriander leaves

½ tbsp. lemon juice

2 tbsp. oil

Salt to taste

1 tbsp. husk mixed with a pinch of salt and ¼ tsp. red chilli powder

Bringing everything together

1. Wash and clean the fish properly.
2. Mix the garlic paste, red chilli and turmeric powders, lemon juice, salt and coriander leaves. Coat the fish pieces with the mixture. Leave them aside for twenty minutes for marination.
3. Heat oil in a pan. Coat the fish pieces in the husk and red chilli powder mix and put them in the pan.
4. Cover the pan with a lid for a few minutes. Once the fish is fried and crispy on one side, remove the lid, flip the fish pieces and let it cook on the other side so that both sides are equally crispy.
5. Drizzle some lemon juice and serve with onion rings.

Nutritional Information Per Serving

Serving Size – 1

Amount Per Serving

Calories 348

Total Fat 30 g

Total Carbohydrate 1 g

Protein 23 g

SNACKS AND SIDES

Cauliflower Tikkis

If you crave for tikkis and think that you cannot enjoy them on Keto diet, say hello to cauliflower tikkis. You won't miss aloo tikkis at all once you make these tikkis using similar Indian spices.

Ingredients:

200 gms riced cauliflower

1 egg (you can replace the egg with 2 tbsp. of husk for binding)

½ cup finely chopped onions

1 tsp. ginger paste

1 tsp. garlic paste

½ tsp. finely chopped green chillies

¼ tsp. turmeric powder

1 tsp. red chilli powder

1tsp. garam masala

¼ tsp. chaat masala

2 tbsp. coriander leaves

2 tbsp. olive oil

2 tbsp. full-fat hung curd or full-fat Greek yoghurt

Salt to taste

Bringing everything together

1. Put the riced cauliflower in a muslin cloth and squeeze out all the water. Shift the dried-out cauliflower to a bowl.

2. Add the masalas, ginger and garlic paste, egg and coriander leaves and mix well. Make a small round ball using the mixture and flatten it in the palm of your hand. Repeat the process till the entire mixture has been used.

3. Heat up oil in a pan and add the tikkis to it once the oil is hot. Shallow fry the tikkis till they are golden brown and crisp.

4. Add a pinch of red chilli powder and chaat masala to the
    hung curd and serve it with the tikkis.

Nutritional Information Per Serving
Serving Size – 2

Amount Per Serving
Calories 230
Total Fat 16 g
Total Carbohydrate 12 g
Protein 12 g

Kurkure Paneer Slices

This quick recipe is a saviour during hunger pangs. You can marinate extra paneer for this recipe and refrigerate it for later use.

Ingredients

100 gms paneer (cut into thick slices)

2 tsp. ginger-garlic paste

2 tbsp. full-fat Greek yoghurt

1 ½ tsp. red chilli powder

1 tsp. turmeric powder

1 tsp. garam masala powder

½ tsp. crushed Kasuri methi

½ tsp. dried mango powder

2 tbsp. finely chopped coriander leaves

2 tbsp. butter or ghee

½ tsp. chaat masala

1 tbsp. lemon juice

Onion rings for garnish

Salt to taste

Bringing everything together

1. Marinate the paneer slices with the yoghurt and all the masalas and keep aside for half an hour.

2. Heat up a pan. Put in butter or ghee. Then add the paneer slices and shallow fry on low to medium heat till golden and crispy.

3. Sprinkle the chaat masala and lemon juice on the paneer slices and garnish with onion rings.

Nutritional Information Per Serving
Serving Size – 2

Amount Per Serving
Calories 298
Total Fat 26 g
Total Carbohydrate 2 g
Protein 11 g

Soya Paneer Cheese Kababs

The easily available soya nuggets are a good source of protein. This recipe uses soya nuggets along with paneer and cheese to make wholesome kababs.

Ingredients

    50 gms soya nuggets (boiled, well drained and mashed or chopped up in a food processor)
    100 gms crumbled paneer
    50 gms grated cheese
    1 ½ tbsp. ginger-garlic paste
    1 tsp. finely chopped green chillies
    2 tbsp. husk
    2 tsp. garam masala
    2 tsp chaat masala
    2 tbsp finely chopped coriander leaves
    Salt to taste
    3 tbsp. ghee or oil or butter to shallow fry

Bringing everything together

1. In a bowl, mix all the ingredients and make flat kababs.
2. Heat up a little oil, ghee or butter in a shallow pan and fry the kababs till they are crispy.
3. Drain them on a paper towel and serve with either cream cheese or hung curd sprinkled with some chaat masala.

Nutritional Information Per Serving

Serving Size – 3

Amount Per Serving

Calories 332

Total Fat 27g

Total Carbohydrate 3 g

Protein 27 g

Palak Methi Roti

Roti and rice are staple foods in Indian cuisine so of course, there is a roti recipe in the list for the Indian Keto followers. You can also add crumbled paneer, chopped onions, caraway seeds (ajwain), ginger or spring onions to the mix.

Ingredients

    1 cup powdered flaxseed
    1 tbsp. husk
    ½ cup chopped methi and spinach (palak) leaves
    1 tsp. garlic-green chilli paste
    1 finely chopped green chilli
    ½ tsp. turmeric powder
    ½ tsp. red chilli powder
    ½ tsp. garam masala
    1 tbsp. oil
    2 tbsp. ghee
    Salt to taste
    Almond or coconut flour for dusting (optional)
    1 cup warm water

Bringing everything together

1. In a big bowl, add the powdered flaxseed, husk, methi and spinach (palak) leaves, garlic-green chilli paste and the dry masalas. Mix everything well and add the oil.

2. Starting off with 1/3 cup of warm water, slowly knead the mixture into a dough, adding more water as needed. Keep it aside for 15–20 minutes.

3. Divide the dough and roll out the rotis using almond or coconut flour.

4. Transfer to a tava on medium heat and cook with ghee till both sides are evenly done.

Nutritional Information Per Serving
Serving Size – 3

Amount Per Serving
Calories 279
Total Fat 28 g
Total Carbohydrate 1 g
Protein 9 g

Gobhi Paranthas

Do you find yourself dreaming of ghee and butter laden paranthas as you are adjusting to the Keto diet? Here is a Keto recipe for paranthas to take care of those cravings. Make a batch of these gobhi paranthas with soya flour and serve them with some butter or yoghurt.

Ingredients

    1 cup soya flour
    ½ cup grated cauliflower
    1 tsp. finely chopped green chillies
    1 tsp. finely chopped ginger
    1 tsp. garam masala
    1 tbsp. oil
    2 tbsp. ghee
    salt to taste
    ¾-1 cup warm water

Bringing everything together

1. Make a mixture of grated cauliflower, green chillies, ginger and garam masala.

2. Make a dough using the soya flour, oil and warm water. Make sure that you add the water slowly while making the dough.

3. Divide the dough into the number of paranthas you want to make. Ensure that each dough ball is large enough to hold the filling.

4. Roll the dough into a small circle and place the cauliflower filling in the centre. Bring all the edges together and join them. Flatten the dough and roll gently using dry flour for dusting.

5. Transfer to a tava on medium heat and cook with ghee
    till both sides are evenly done. Serve with white butter or
    yoghurt.

Nutritional Information Per Serving
Serving Size – 2

Amount Per Serving
Calories 246
Total Fat 22 g
Total Carbohydrate 3 g
Protein 7 g

Palak Raita

My mother-in-law introduced me to this recipe and I have loved it ever since. This is a great accompaniment to paranthas, pulao and can even be served as a dip with spicy tikkis.

Ingredients

2 cups spinach
1 cup full-fat Greek yoghurt
1 tbsp. ghee
1–2 slit green chillies
4–5 curry leaves
¼ tsp. asafoetida
½ tsp. cumin seeds
¼ tsp. cumin powder
Salt to taste

Bringing everything together

1. Fill a saucepan halfway with water and let it boil. Add some salt to it and afterwards, add the washed spinach. Cook the spinach till it wilts.

2. Drain the liquid using a colander and let the spinach cool for a few minutes.

3. Squeeze out the additional water and chop the spinach.

4. Mix the spinach and yoghurt and add salt to season.

5. In a small tadka pan, heat up the ghee. As it melts, add the cumin seeds and let them splutter. Add the slit green chillies and curry leaves and let them splutter as well and once they have been roasted in the ghee, add the asafoetida.

6. Add this tadka seasoning to the spinach and yoghurt mix and blend everything well. Sprinkle the roasted cumin powder over the raita.

Tip: Always keep some cumin powder handy to dress up raitas. You can also jazz up some yoghurt with roasted cumin powder, red chilli powder and black salt to serve with rotis or paranthas.

Nutritional Information Per Serving
Serving Size – 2

Amount Per Serving
Calories 229
Total Fat 20 g
Total Carbohydrate 4 g
Protein 10 g

Seedhi-Saadhi Bhindi

I always keep some bhindi (lady's finger/okra) in the refrigerator since it is one of the few vegetables that my children eat. Yes, I also belong to the 'mother of picky-eaters' club. So this recipe is perfect for the parents following the Keto diet and their kids.

Ingredients

    250 gms bhindi
    2 tbsp. ghee
    ¼ tsp asafoetida
    ½ tsp. cumin seeds
    1 tsp. red chilli powder
    ½ tsp. turmeric powder
    1 tsp. roasted coriander and cumin powder
    ½ tsp dried mango powder
    Salt to taste

Bringing everything together

1. Wash the bhindi thoroughly, dry it on a kitchen towel and cut into either small round pieces or large slices.

2. Put some ghee in a pan on medium heat and add cumin seeds to it. Let them splutter.

3. Reduce the heat and add asafoetida, turmeric, red chilli and coriander-cumin powders to the ghee.

4. Then add the bhindi to the pan and slowly increase the heat. Keep stirring till the bhindi is fried and has mixed well with the spices. Season with salt.

5. If you'd like the bhindi to be slightly crispy, make sure to cook it for about 15–20 minutes on medium to low heat. Keep stirring in between.

6. If you'd like it to be slightly soft, cook for about 12 minutes or so until it is done.

7. Before serving the dish, sprinkle dried mango powder on it and mix well.

Tip: This recipe works like a charm for dahi-bhindi as well. Make sure you cook the bhindi till it is crisp and once slightly cooled, add the desired amount to a bowl of full-fat Greek yoghurt and sprinkle with some chaat masala, salt and red chilli powder.

Nutritional Information Per Serving
Serving Size – 2

Amount Per Serving
Calories 188
Total Fat 15 g
Total Carbohydrate 7 g
Protein 3 g

Kick-start your weight loss journey by joining our 7-day challenge at https://www.ketomonk.com/bonus.

Vaangi Kaap

Vaangi Kaap (thinly sliced brinjal) is a nice accompaniment to a rice dish and is extremely easy to make. You can keep the brinjal pieces soft or slightly crispy depending on how you like them.

Ingredients

1 medium sized brinjal

2 tsp. red chilli powder

1 tsp. turmeric powder

2 tsp. coriander and cumin powder

½ tsp. garam masala

1 tbsp. flaxseed meal

¼ cup finely chopped fresh coriander leaves

3 tbsp. olive oil

¼ tsp. sweetener (optional)

Salt to taste

Bringing everything together

1. Wash the brinjal and cut into slices. Keep the thickness of the slices at half an inch.

2. Mix the dry spices powders with the flaxseed meal and season with salt. The sweetener is optional.

3. Add a few teaspoons of water to the mixture to form a paste like consistency.

4. Apply the spice mixture only on one side of all the brinjal slices.

5. Heat up a tablespoon of oil in a shallow pan on medium heat and gently slide the brinjal slices in with the spice mixture side on the top. Drizzle the slices with some of the oil, cover the pan and cook until the brinjal slices turn a little brown on the bottom and soften.

6. Flip the slices and cook the other side until crispy. Keep
    drizzling the oil so that the brinjal slices don't burn and
    stick to the pan.

Tip: You can use the same spice mix for lauki, bottle gourd or opo
squash and follow the same recipe.

Nutritional Information Per Serving
Serving Size – 2

Amount Per Serving
Calories 192
Total Fat 20 g
Total Carbohydrate 1 g
Protein 0 g

Mooli Raita

Mooli (henceforth referred to as radish) is another low-carb vegetable that is easily available and this raita is a good accompaniment to paranthas and pulao.

Ingredients

100 gms. radish of any kind
1 cup. full-fat hung curd or full-fat Greek yoghurt
½ tsp. cumin seeds
¼ tsp. asafoetida
1 tbsp. finely chopped fresh coriander leaves
2 tsp. ghee
1 tbsp. roasted and coarsely crushed peanuts
1 green chilli sliced lengthwise (remove the seeds if you want to avoid the heat)
½ tsp. cumin seeds powder
Salt to taste

Bringing everything together

1. Clean the radish under running water, trim the ends and peel the skin. You can leave the skin on the radish for cooking if you are using small red radishes.

2. Grate the radish coarsely, add a few pinches of salt and let it sit for a few minutes.

3. Squeeze out the extra liquid and transfer the radish to a bowl. Add the hung curd, fresh coriander leaves and season with salt.

4. In a small sauté pan, heat up the ghee on medium heat.

5. Once it melts, add the cumin seeds and let them splutter. Add the slit green chilli and fry for a minute and then add the asafoetida.

6. Pour this seasoning into the bowl with the radish and blend everything well. Sprinkle with roasted cumin powder.

Tip: You can substitute the radish with cucumbers.

Nutritional Information Per Serving
Serving Size –2

Amount Per Serving
Calories 157
Total Fat 12 g
Total Carbohydrate 4 g
Protein 6 g

Strawberry Smoothie

Smoothies are a great snack to have in between meals. You can replace strawberries with similar seasonal berries. You can also freeze strawberries and use them later.

Ingredients

100 gms unsweetened coconut milk
100 gms strawberries
50 ml fresh cream or heavy cream
Sweetener to taste

Bringing everything together

1. Blend the ingredients together with a couple of ice cubes in the blender and chill before serving.

2. Add sweetener to taste.

Nutritional Information Per Serving
Serving Size – 2

Amount Per Serving
Calories 76
Total Fat 12 g
Total Carbohydrate 4 g
Protein 1 g

Chow Chow Poriyal

Chayote squash used in this recipe is a fairly versatile vegetable and can be used in sabzis, poriyals or to make sambar. It can be cooked quickly and makes for a good side dish.

Ingredients

1 chayote squash (deseeded and cut into cubes)
½ tsp. mustard seeds
1 tbsp. ghee or coconut oil
1 chopped red chilli
5–6 curry leaves
2 tsp. fresh grated coconut
Salt to taste

Bringing everything together

1. In a kadai or pan, heat up ghee/oil and when hot, add the mustard seeds till they splutter.
2. Add the red chilli and the curry leaves and fry till the chilli becomes slightly dark.
3. Add the chayote squash, salt and little water. Cover the pan and cook.
4. Let the squash cook for ten to twelve minutes.
5. Garnish with the fresh grated coconut and serve.

Tip: If you prefer a slightly spicy version then add some turmeric powder, red chilli powder and a pinch of garam masala to the dish.

Nutritional Information Per Serving
Serving Size – 2

Amount Per Serving
Calories 105
Total Fat 9 g
Total Carbohydrate 3 g
Protein 1 g

Methi Theplas

When methi (fresh fenugreek) is in season, like a vast majority of methi lovers, I end up using it in theplas, paranthas, sabzis and pulao.

Ingredients

¼ cup flaxseed meal
1 tbsp. husk
¼ cup almond flour
½ cup soya flour
1 tbsp. unsweetened, desiccated coconut
1 tsp. turmeric powder
1 finely chopped green chilli
1/2 tsp. finely chopped ginger
1 cup chopped methi leaves
¼ full-fat yoghurt or hung curd
1 tsp. sesame seeds
2 tbsp. melted ghee
½ tsp. salt
Water as required to make the dough

Bringing everything together

1. In a bowl, mix together the flaxseed meal, husk, almond flour, soya flour, desiccated coconut, ginger, green chilli, turmeric powder, salt and sesame seeds.

2. Add the yoghurt and bind the dough. Add water as needed to make the dough slightly soft. You can also add some of the melted ghee to bring the dough together. Let it rest for a few minutes.

3. Put a flat-bottomed pan or tava on medium heat. Make balls of the dough and roll out the theplas using a little soya flour for dusting if needed.

4. Transfer the thepla one at a time to the pan and use the melted ghee for greasing. Cook until both sides are brown and done. Serve with a raita, a vegetable or meat dish.

Nutritional Information Per Serving

Serving Size – 2

Amount Per Serving

Calories 455

Total Fat 35 g

Total Carbohydrate 11 g

Protein 17 g

Baingan Bharta

This much-loved Indian dish clearly needs no introduction. It can be served as a side dish with rotis and paranthas.

Ingredients

1 medium sized to slightly big sized baingan (brinjal)
¼ cup finely chopped onions
¼ cup finely chopped tomatoes
1 finely chopped green chilli
½ tsp. cumin seeds
½ tsp. finely grated ginger
½ tsp. turmeric powder
1 tsp. red chilli powder
½ tsp. garam masala powder
½ tsp. coriander powder
1 tbsp. finely chopped fresh coriander leaves
2 tbsp. ghee
1 tbsp. butter
Just enough oil to coat the brinjal before roasting
Salt to taste

Bringing everything together

1. Wash the brinjal and apply oil on it. Prick it with a fork in three to four places.
2. Roast the brinjal over the stovetop. Keep turning it constantly till the entire brinjal is blistered, charred and completely roasted.
3. Alternatively, you can roast the brinjal in a convection oven at about 180 degrees Celsius/350 degrees Fahrenheit for about half an hour.

4. Once the brinjal is roasted and cooled, slowly peel off the skin to remove the burnt part. Chop the flesh of the brinjal roughly and keep it aside.

5. In a pan, heat the ghee and splutter the cumin seeds.

6. Add the green chilli and fry for a few seconds.

7. Next, add the onions and ginger and cook till the onions turn slightly brown. At this point, add the tomatoes and cook till they soften.

8. Add the spice powders to the pan.

9. Cook for a minute. Add the chopped brinjal and season with salt.

10. Blend everything well together and sprinkle a little water. Cover and cook for about five minutes.

11. Add the butter and mix everything once again and garnish with finely chopped coriander leaves.

Nutritional Information Per Serving
Serving Size – 2

Amount Per Serving
Calories 198
Total Fat 21 g
Total Carbohydrate 1 g
Protein 1 g

Kurkura Karela

Karela (Bitter gourd) is not a favourite vegetable for many of us. The bitterness of karela is partly to be blamed for that. But this simple recipe is worth trying and may even change your opinion on this interesting vegetable. I love making this as a crispy side dish with curd rice.

Ingredients

200 gms karela
2 tsp. red chilli powder
1 tsp. turmeric powder
1 tsp. coriander powder
½ tsp. asafoetida
2 tbsp ghee
Salt to taste

Bringing everything together

1. Wash the karela, scrape off the skin and cut into slices. You can retain the seeds but that is optional.

2. Sprinkle salt on the slices and let them sit aside for fifteen minutes. This reduces the bitterness. Afterwards, squeeze the slices to remove moisture from the karela.

3. In a pan, heat up ghee and once it is warm, add the asafoetida.

4. Add the karela slices along with the spice powders and season with salt.

5. Mix everything well together and keep cooking on medium heat till all the slices turn crispy. It will take around half an hour to cook but you need to keep stirring it intermittently. Once ready, serve hot with the main dish.

Tip: If you like something crispy with your south Indian meals, in lieu of papad, this serves as a good Keto replacement.

Nutritional Information Per Serving
Serving Size – 2

Amount Per Serving
Calories 260
Total Fat 27 g
Total Carbohydrate 5 g
Protein 1 g

Palak ka Parantha

Spinach (palak) is a nutrient-rich vegetable so you can use this recipe for breakfast to start your day on a high note.

Ingredients

¼ cup flaxseed meal
1 tbsp. husk
¼ cup almond meal
½ cup soya flour
½ cup broccoli florets (steamed for a few minutes and finely grated)
¼ cup chopped spinach
1 finely chopped green chilli
½ tsp. finely chopped ginger
1 finely chopped green onion (with the stalk)
A pinch of garam masala
1 tsp. finely chopped fresh coriander leaves
2 tbsp. melted ghee
½ tsp. salt
Water as required to make the dough

Bringing everything together

1. In a bowl, mix together the flaxseed meal, husk, almond meal, soya flour, broccoli, spinach and green onions, ginger, green chilli, turmeric powder, garam masala, fresh coriander and salt.

2. Add water and start bringing the dough together. Add water as needed to make a slightly soft dough. You can also add some melted ghee to bring the dough together. Let it rest for a few minutes.

3. Put a flat-bottomed pan or tava on medium heat. Make balls of the dough and roll out the paranthas using some soya flour for dusting if needed.

4. Transfer the paranthas one at a time to the pan and use the melted ghee for greasing. Cook until both sides are brown and done.

5. Serve with a raita, a vegetable or meat dish.

Tip: You can use methi leaves if they are in season. You can also add sesame or sesame seeds to the dough.

Nutritional Information Per Serving
Serving Size – 2

Amount Per Serving
Calories 352
Total Fat 27 g
Total Carbohydrate 9 g
Protein 14 g

Tondekai Sabzi (Tondli or Ivy Gourd)

Tondekai (Ivy gourd) is easily available in the market. Make sure to pick the pieces which are green in colour and slightly slender.

Ingredients

250 gms Ivy gourd

2 tsp. roasted sesame seed powder

2 tsp. roasted peanut powder

2 tsp. fresh grated coconut

½ tsp. turmeric powder

2 tsp. red chilli powder

½ tsp asafoetida

1 tsp. cumin and coriander seeds powder

½ tsp. garam masala powder

½ tsp. cumin seeds

2 tbsp. ghee

1 tbsp. finely chopped fresh coriander leaves

Salt for seasoning

Pinch of sweetener (optional)

Bringing everything together

1. Wash the vegetable well and cut off the ends. You can either cut the pieces into long thin slices or into thin round slices.

2. In a thick-bottomed pan or kadhai on medium heat, add the ghee and let it melt. Once melted, add the cumin seeds and let them splutter. Add the asafoetida and let it all fry for a few seconds.

3. Add the vegetable and stir it so that it gets coated with ghee. Cover the pan and let it cook for ten minutes.

4.   Uncover the pan and check to see if the vegetable has softened and been cooked partially.

5.   Once the vegetable is a little under-cooked, add the spice powders, sesame and peanut powders, fresh grated coconut and season with salt. Stir to mix everything together.

6.   Cover the pan and let the dish simmer until the vegetable is completely cooked. If the contents are sticking to the pan, either add some ghee or sprinkle a few drops of water.

7.   Uncover the pan and fry for another 3–4 minutes until the vegetable is dry.

8.   Add a pinch of sweetener if you like a hint of sweetness to your sabzi otherwise the fresh coconut will anyway add a lovely touch. Add the fresh coriander leaves and cook for another minute.

9.   Serve with a roti of your choice.

Tip: While making roasted sesame powder or roasted peanut powder, make a little extra and store it in air tight containers or in the refrigerator so you can use them for other recipes too. Just roast them slightly and coarsely grind them in a blender.

Nutritional Information Per Serving
Serving Size – 2

Amount Per Serving
Calories 201
Total Fat 18 g
Total Carbohydrate 3 g
Protein 3 g

Keerai Masiyal

Keerai Masiyal is made with mashed greens. Growing up, my
mother cooked a variety of them and I would eat them with
rice and a big dollop of ghee. A wide variety of greens are easily
available in the Indian markets. This recipe uses spinach but you
can use whichever green leafy vegetables you prefer. Some recipes
don't use coconut but to make this recipe more Keto friendly, I
have included coconut.

Ingredients

1 big bunch of spinach leaves
2 tbsp. fresh grated coconut
2–3 small onions (cut into halves)
2 cloves of garlic
½ tsp. cumin seeds and ¼ extra for tempering
2 long dried red chillies
½ tsp. turmeric powder
½ tsp. mustard seeds
¼ tsp. asafoetida
2 tbsp. ghee or coconut oil
Salt to taste

Bringing everything together

1. Clean the spinach leaves and discard stems that are thick
   or not tender. After washing the spinach, roughly chop it
   up and keep aside.
2. In a pan on heat, add one tbsp. of the ghee and splutter ½
   tsp. of cumin seeds.
3. Add the onion and garlic and fry for a few minutes.
4. Next, add the chopped spinach and the turmeric powder
   and cook until the spinach completely wilts and is done. It
   will also release some water.

5. As the spinach is cooking, grind one red chilli and the
    fresh grated coconut using very little water in the blender
    and keep aside.

6. Once the spinach is cooked, let it cool for a few minutes
    and using a blender, coarsely grind the spinach mixture.
    You can keep the consistency as smooth or as coarse as
    you prefer.

7. Transfer the spinach mixture back to the pan which has
    some of the water released by the spinach while cooking.
    Then add the ground coconut and red chilli and mix
    everything well.

8. Season with salt and let it cook for 3–4 minutes.

9. In a small pan or tempering pan, heat the remaining ghee
    or coconut oil and add the ¼ tsp of cumin seeds, mustard
    seeds and let them splutter. Add the other dried red chilli
    and asafoetida. Add this tempering to the spinach.

10. Serve this with either coconut cauliflower rice or as a
    side dish.

Nutritional Information Per Serving
Serving Size – 2

Amount Per Serving
Calories 230
Total Fat 17 g
Total Carbohydrate 8 g
Protein 5 g

Coconut Chutney

This easy coconut recipe can be served with dosa or coconut rice.

Ingredients

 1 cup fresh grated coconut
 1 green chilli
 ½ tsp. mustard seeds
 ¼ tsp. asafoetida
 8–10 fresh curry leaves
 1 tsp. peanuts
 1 ½ tsp. coconut oil
 1 tbsp. finely chopped coriander leaves
 1 tsp. chopped ginger
 Salt to season

Bringing everything together

1. Blend together the fresh grated coconut, green chilli, peanuts, coriander leaves and ginger with very little water. Season with salt and transfer to a bowl.

2. In a small tempering pan, heat up the coconut oil and splutter the mustard seeds. Add the asafoetida and curry leaves and pour this tempering over the chutney.

Nutritional Information Per Serving
Serving Size – 2

Amount Per Serving
Calories 238
Total Fat 23 g
Total Carbohydrate 4 g
Protein 3 g

Pumpkin Raita

This delicious raita is a wonderful accompaniment to rotis and paranthas.

Ingredients

    100 gms pumpkin
    1 cup full-fat Greek yoghurt or full-fat hung curd
    ½ cup sour cream
    1 tsp. roasted and crushed peanut powder
    1 green chilli (slit lengthwise)
    4–5 curry leaves
    1 tsp. cumin seeds
    1 tsp. ghee
    ¼ tsp. asafoetida
    1 tbsp. finely chopped fresh coriander leaves
    Pinch of sweetener
    Salt to taste

Bringing everything together

1. Peel the pumpkin and cut it into big cubes. Cook the pumpkin with very little water either in the pressure cooker or in the microwave till it softens. Make sure that it isn't too mushy.

2. Once it cools down, grate the pumpkin.

3. Add the yoghurt or hung curd, sour cream, peanut powder, salt, sweetner and the fresh coriander. Mix everything well together.

4. In a small tempering pan, heat up the ghee and splutter the cumin seeds. Add the green chilli, curry leaves and the asafoetida and fry for a few seconds. Add this tempering to the raita and serve.

Nutritional Information Per Serving
Serving Size – 3

Amount Per Serving
Calories 201
Total Fat 15 g
Total Carbohydrate 9 g
Protein 8 g

Get additional bonus material and access to a 7-day challenge by signing up at https://www.ketomonk.com/bonus.

Broccoli Paneer Tikkis

This recipe uses broccoli but if it isn't easily available, you can always use cauliflower as a substitute.

Ingredients

    1 cup finely crumbled or grated paneer
    2 cups cooked and grated broccoli
    3 tsp. psyllium husk
    2 tsp. finely chopped ginger
    2 tsp. finely chopped green chillies
    2 tsp. chaat masala
    1 tsp. garlic powder
    2 tbsp. finely chopped fresh coriander leaves
    3 tbsp. ghee for shallow frying
    Salt and pepper to taste

Bringing everything together

1. In a bowl, combine the paneer, broccoli, husk, ginger, green chillies, chaat masala, garlic powder, fresh coriander and season with salt and pepper.

2. Take some mixture in your palms, roll and flatten it into a disc. Repeat this process with the remaining mixture.

3. In a pan, melt the ghee and shallow fry the tikkis. Once the tikki fries on one side, flip it to cook evenly on both sides.

4. Serve with a mint chutney or a dip of your choice.

Tip: You can always add vegetables like spinach or grated cheese to the recipe that fit within your macros.

Nutritional Information Per Serving

Serving Size – 2

Amount Per Serving

Calories 326

Total Fat 29 g

Total Carbohydrate 3 g

Protein 7 g

Cucumber Peanut Salad

This easy salad can be made as a side or as a snack. The peanuts add a nice crunch. It is a good idea to keep some roasted peanut powder at home to sprinkle on salads or desserts. For the peanut powder, roast the peanuts in a pan on medium heat so that the skin blackens slightly. Let the peanuts cool down and remove the skins. Use a mortar and pestle or a quick turn in the mixer to coarsely grind the peanuts.

Ingredients

50 gms diced cucumber
1 tbsp. roasted peanut powder
1 tsp. oil
A pinch of asafoetida
½ tsp. cumin seeds
1 slit green chilli
1 tbsp. lemon juice
1 tbsp. finely chopped coriander leaves
3–4 curry leaves
1/2 tsp. sweetener
Salt to taste

Bringing everything together

1. In a bowl, mix together the cucumber, peanut powder, lemon juice, salt and sweetener.

2. In a small tadka or tempering pan, heat up the oil, add asafoetida and cumin seeds. Once the cumin seeds splutter, add the slit green chilli and curry leaves. Add this tadka to the salad mixture and mix well.

3. Garnish with chopped coriander leaves.

Nutritional Information Per Serving

Serving Size – 1

Amount Per Serving

Calories 101

Total Fat 9 g

Total Carbohydrate 3 g

Protein 3 g

DESSERTS

Paneer Pick-Me-Ups

These small laddoos can be prepared in advance and refrigerated. You can enjoy them as snacks or dessert.

Ingredients

100 gms paneer
1 scoop whey (whichever flavour you prefer)
25 gms almonds
25 ml almond milk
Few strands of saffron
A pinch of cardamom powder
2 tsp. of ghee to grease palms
Sweetener to taste

Bringing everything together

1. Grind the nuts coarsely in a blender for a couple of minutes or chop them coarsely and keep aside.

2. In a blender, blend the paneer, whey, almond milk, saffron and cardamom powder together. Make sure that there are no lumps and it turns into a soft mixture.

3. If you don't have almond milk, use either cream or a few drops of water to blend the paneer and whey.

4. Put the mixture in a bowl and add the nuts.

5. Grease your palms with ghee and roll the mixture into small round balls or laddoos.

6. Refrigerate the laddoos for a couple of hours before serving.

Tip: You can also roll these in desiccated coconut to add some crunch and flavour. You can also add a few drops of food colouring to make them vibrant.

Nutritional Information Per Serving
Serving Size – 4

Amount Per Serving
Calories 178
Total Fat 13 g
Total Carbohydrate 1 g
Protein 13 g

If you are on Keto diet, take your weight loss journey to the next level with Intermittent Fasting. You can sign up for the 7-day challenge for FREE at https://www.ketomonk.com/bonus.

Lassi

Lassi can be served as a nice summer beverage. You can have it in between meals. If you aren't fond of the sweet lassi then you can blend the yoghurt with bit of ginger, fresh coriander leaves, green chillies, ice, salt to taste and top it off with cumin powder.

Ingredients

100 gms full-fat Greek yoghurt
¼ cup full-fat cream
Sweetener to taste
A pinch of ground cardamom powder
Salt
1 tsp. almonds or Keto approved nuts
Ice as needed

Bringing everything together

1. Blend all the ingredients in a blender along with the ice. You can make a big batch and refrigerate it for later use. You can either blend the cream with the yoghurt or top the lassi with cream.

Tip: Whenever different seasonal berries are available, you can add a handful of them to the lassi while blending the ingredients. Make sure the berries fall within your macros.

Nutritional Information Per Serving
Serving Size – 2

Amount Per Serving
Calories 172
Total Fat 15 g
Total Carbohydrate 4 g
Protein 6 g

Shrikhand

For many of us, shrikhand evokes festive memories and rightfully so. This simple yet creamy dessert has always been a part of menus during festivals and ceremonies and thankfully, it can be adapted to a Ketogenic diet as well. Greek yoghurt, if available, can be used directly or you can use full-fat hung curd. Hung curd can be made by straining full-fat curd in a muslin cloth or by using a fine strainer until the water drains out.

Ingredients

100 gms full-fat Greek yoghurt or full-fat hung curd

3 tbsp. almond milk

2 tbsp. chopped nuts

A few strands of saffron

½ tsp. cardamom powder (optional)

2 tbsp. sweetener to taste

Bringing everything together

1. Warm the almond milk and dissolve the saffron strands in it.

2. In a bowl, carefully blend the yoghurt, two teaspoons of the saffron infused almond milk, chopped nuts, cardamom powder and the sweetener using a spoon or a spatula.

3. Chill for a couple of hours in the refrigerator and serve.

Nutritional Information Per Serving
Serving Size – 2

Amount Per Serving
Calories 444
Total Fat 33g
Total Carbohydrate 7 g
Protein 29 g

Lauki ki Kheer

As children, a lot of us probably fussed over having to eat lauki (Bottle gourd) for a meal. This disliked vegetable is full of nutrition and can be masqueraded in a lot of ways. Try this sweet version if the savory ones are not for you.

Ingredients

150 gms lauki (grated)

100 gms heavy cream

25 gms ghee

1 tbsp. sweetener or as per taste

2 tbsp. nuts crushed with a few strands of saffron

Bringing everything together

1. The grated lauki will release a fair bit of water so squeeze out all the moisture using a kitchen towel or napkin.

2. In a thick-bottomed pan, heat up the ghee and add the lauki. Let it cook for 6–7 minutes.

3. Add the cream and let it cook on a low to medium flame for ten minutes. Keep stirring so that it does not burn. The kheer should have a much thicker consistency after ten minutes.

4. Add the sweetener and the nuts (reserve some for topping) and cook for another couple of minutes. If it looks like the kheer has thickened too much at this point, you can add a little water.

5. You can serve this warm or once cooled, you can refrigerate it and serve later. Garnish with the reserved mixed nuts.

Tip: You can crush the almonds with a few strands of saffron. Reserve some for the topping.

Nutritional Information Per Serving

Serving Size – 3

Amount Per Serving

Calories 247

Total Fat 23 g

Total Carbohydrate 9 g

Protein 2 g

Kesar Kalakand

Kalakand, a favourite Indian dessert, can be easily replicated at home. Whenever you crave for this desi mithai, you can make this Keto version of kalakand which is an equally tasty but a healthier option.

Ingredients

200 gms crumbled paneer
50 ml almond milk
50 ml fresh cream
½ tsp. cardamom powder
2 tbsp. mixed nuts
2 tbsp. ghee + 2 tsp. for greasing a tray
1 tbsp. saffron dissolved in 2 tbsp. warm almond milk
3 tbsp. sweetener or as per taste

Bringing everything together

1. In a heavy-bottomed pan, heat up the ghee and add the paneer. Cook for 3–4 minutes.

2. Add the almond milk and fresh cream and cook till the mixture comes together and thickens.

3. Add the cardamom powder and the saffron dissolved in the almond milk and mix so that the mixture is evenly coloured with the saffron.

4. Turn off the heat and spread the kalakand on a tray or plate that has been greased with ghee.

5. Spread the mixed nuts all over the kalakand and gently press them down. Let the dish cool down to room temperature and then chill for a couple of hours. Cut into squares and store in the refrigerator.

Nutritional Information Per Serving

Serving Size – 4

Amount Per Serving

Calories 348

Total Fat 28 g

Total Carbohydrate 10 g

Protein 12 g

Aliv Seeds Kheer

Aliv (also known as Garden Cress or Halim) seeds are extremely nutritious and aliv laddoos are healthy as well. I ate them a lot post pregnancy because of their health benefits and I am glad that we can continue to use them on Keto diet as well. Make sure you refrigerate the leftovers since the recipe contains fresh coconut. These seeds, once soaked, resemble basil seeds.

Ingredients

2 tbsp. aliv seeds (garden cress or halim)
2 cups unsweetened coconut milk
1 cup fresh grated coconut
¼ tsp. nutmeg powder
1 tbsp. coarsely pounded almonds
1 tbsp. ghee
Few strands of saffron
Sweetener to taste

Bringing everything together

1. Soak the seeds in half a cup of unsweetened coconut milk for about 2–3 hours. The seeds will swell up and have a jelly like consistency.

2. In a pan on low to medium heat, melt the ghee and add the coconut and cook for 3–4 minutes.

3. Add the remaining coconut milk and cook for another 4–5 minutes, stirring continuously.

4. Next, add the soaked aliv seeds (after discarding the coconut milk in which the seeds were soaked), nutmeg powder, almonds, saffron and sweetener.

5. You can taste the mixture at this stage to adjust amount of sweetener in it. Cook for a few more minutes until

all the ingredients are blended well and it comes to a slow boil.

6. Take it off the stove and serve hot.

Nutritional Information Per Serving
Serving Size – 3

Amount Per Serving
Calories 191
Total Fat 19 g
Total Carbohydrate 5 g
Protein 2 g

Til Barfi

Til or sesame seeds are nutrient rich and allowed on Keto. While it is easy to incorporate them into vegetables and rotis, making a dessert is another way to enjoy them. The traditional tilachi vadi or til laddoos use jaggery and sugar which we have replaced with sweeteners in this recipe.

Ingredients

   1 cup til or sesame seeds
   ¼ cup roasted peanut powder
   ¼ cup powdered almonds (slightly coarse)
   ¼ cup desiccated coconut
   1 tbsp. almond flour
   3 tbsp. ghee (reserve one tsp. for greasing)
   ½ tbsp. powdered sweetener or according to taste

Bringing everything together

1. Dry roast the til or sesame seeds for about 4–5 minutes. Make sure that they don't burn.

2. Coarsely grind them in a blender or in a mortar and pestle.

3. Melt ghee in a pan on heat and add the sesame powder, peanut powder, powdered almonds, desiccated coconut and the almond flour.

4. Add the sweetener according to taste. Mix all the ingredients well and cook for about 7–8 minutes till they are well-blended. Adjust the quantity of ghee and almond flour as needed so that everything binds well together.

5. Grease a plate or tray with ghee, transfer this mixture to it and press it down so that it is tightly packed.

6. Cut into shapes of your choice and let it cool down. You can refrigerate it for sometime as well so that it sets and is easier to cut.

Tip: You can add different nuts to the mix or sprinkle some pumpkin or sunflower seeds to add some extra crunch.

Nutritional Information Per Serving
Serving Size – 6

Amount Per Serving
Calories 261
Total Fat 24 g
Total Carbohydrate 5 g
Protein 6 g

Paneer Phirni

This quick dessert can be made in advance and refrigerated in batches to be enjoyed more than once. Traditional phirni uses ground rice but it is replaced with paneer in this recipe.

Ingredients

1 cup heavy cream
¼ cup finely crumbled paneer
½ cup almond milk
1 tbsp. chopped almonds
Few strands of saffron
¼ tsp. ground cardamom powder
1 tbsp. sweetener

Bringing everything together

1. Put a pan on low heat and add the heavy cream and almond milk and slowly mix them together with either a whisk or a spoon till it all blends well.

2. Add the finely crumbled paneer and keep stirring for a few more minutes. The mixture will become slightly thick.

3. Keep stirring continuously so as to avoid lumps and prevent the mixture from burning.

4. Add the sweetener, saffron and the ground cardamom powder and stir for another couple of minutes. Adjust the sweetener according to your preference.

5. Take the pan off the heat and let it cool down.

6. Transfer the phirni into individual bowls and refrigerate for about 3–4 hours and enjoy it cold.

Nutritional Information Per Serving

Serving Size – 3

Amount Per Serving

Calories 331

Total Fat 32 g

Total Carbohydrate 5 g

Protein 2 g

If you are thinking of starting the Keto diet, we would highly recommend starting with Intermittent Fasting and then getting on the Keto diet. Take the 7-day free challenge at https://www.ketomonk.com/bonus.

Gulabi Kulfi

Gulabi kulfi gets its name and colour from the berries used in the recipe. Use whatever berries you have on hand and freeze a batch while you are at it.

Ingredients

200 ml. fresh cream
1 cup full-fat yoghurt
¼ cup strawberries
1 tsp. unsweetened rose essence
Sweetener to taste

Bringing everything together

1. Blend all the ingredients in a food processor or use a hand blender.
2. Fill the kulfi molds and freeze overnight.

Nutritional Information Per Serving
Serving Size – 3

Amount Per Serving
Calories 256
Total Fat 20 g
Total Carbohydrate 10 g
Protein 8 g

Chocolate Barfi

If you remember the barfi from your childhood which had two layers of chocolate and khoya filling, you will enjoy this recipe. Though it isn't an exact replica, it will still do the job of satisfying the sweet tooth. The recipe contains a small amount of finely chopped pistachios as a reminder of the barfis I ate as a child but you can always replace them with walnuts as they are heavier in carbs as long as that fits within your macros.

Ingredients

½ cup butter softened to room temperature

100 gms. soft cream cheese

2 tbsp. unsweetened dark cocoa powder

1–2 tbsp. sweetener (or according to taste)

1 tsp. of finely chopped pistachios

2–3 drops of unsweetened rose essence

Bringing everything together

1. Mix the butter and cream cheese gently with a spatula until it becomes smooth and contains no lumps.

2. Add the cocoa powder, sweetener and the rose essence drops and mix well so that they are all blended together with the butter and cream cheese mixture.

3. Line a small tray or plate with parchment or wax or butter paper. Spread the mixture on the tray and flatten it.

4. Sprinkle the crushed pistachios over the mixture and refrigerate for about three hours or until it is set well.

5. Cut into squares and serve.

Nutritional Information Per Serving

Serving Size – 4

Amount Per Serving

Calories 306

Total Fat 33 g

Total Carbohydrate 3 g

Protein 3 g

Chocolate Paneer Laddoos

Make a batch of these and enjoy them as bite-sized treats.

Ingredients

1 cup crumbled paneer
½ cup cream cheese
1 tbsp. unsweetened cocoa powder
Sweetener to taste
1 tbsp. sliced or crushed almonds
1 tsp. ghee for greasing palms
1 tbsp. desiccated coconut

Bringing everything together

1. In a blender, slowly blend together the crumbled paneer, cocoa powder, sweetener, crushed almonds and cream cheese to create a dense and even mixture.

2. Using a spatula, transfer the mixture to a bowl. Grease your palms with ghee and using a little mixture at a time, make tiny balls of equal size.

3. Roll them in the desiccated coconut and refrigerate for some time before serving.

Tip: You can add walnuts or other nuts as per your preference to the laddoos to add more crunch and texture.

Nutritional Information Per Serving
Serving Size – 4

Amount Per Serving
Calories 344
Total Fat 29 g
Total Carbohydrate 4 g
Protein 15 g

Coconut and Cream Barfi

Coconut and Cream Barfi is made using desiccated coconut and fresh cream with a faint hint of cardamom. You can always add nuts of your choice while making the barfis or just garnish them with nuts.

Ingredients

1 cup unsweetened, desiccated coconut
¼ cup fresh cream (you can also use the tetra pack version)
2 tbsp. unsweetened coconut milk
Sweetener to taste
½ tbsp. ghee for greasing
2 tbsp. mixed nuts (optional)
½ tsp. cardamom powder (optional)

Bringing everything together

1. Put a pan to heat and add the desiccated coconut, cream, coconut milk, sweetener, nuts and the cardamom powder. Mix everything so that all the ingredients blend together.

2. Keep stirring on medium heat till the mixture starts thickening and begins to leave the edges of the pan. This may take about 12–15 minutes.

3. Grease a plate or tray with ghee and evenly pour the mixture onto it. If you are using the nuts as topping, spread them at this stage on top of the mixture. Let it cool and then cut the set mixture into squares. Make sure to store the leftovers in the refrigerator.

Nutritional Information Per Serving
Serving Size – 3

Amount Per Serving
Calories 359
Total Fat 32 g
Total Carbohydrate 11 g
Protein 1 g

Chocolate and Coffee Ice Cream

Chocolate and coffee are often a much-loved pair but if coffee is not for you, skip the coffee and make yourself some good old chocolate ice cream.

Ingredients

200 ml fresh cream
2 tbsp. chocolate flavoured whey
2 tbsp. unsweetened cocoa powder
1 tsp. instant coffee powder (dissolved in 1 tbsp. warm water and cooled)
1 tbsp. vanilla essence
2 tbsp. mixed nuts (optional)
Sweetener to taste

Bringing everything together

1. Blend all the fresh cream, whey, cocoa powder and the coffee decoction in a blender or whisk till everything is mixed well. The mixture should be smooth and thick in consistency.

2. Pour it into a container and top with mixed nuts. Freeze for a few hours.

Nutritional Information Per Serving
Serving Size – 2

Amount Per Serving
Calories 198
Total Fat 17 g
Total Carbohydrate 8 g
Protein 6 g

Nariyal Malai Laddoos

These coconut, cream and masala whey laddoos are a quick fix for your cravings. If you can't find milk masala whey, you can substitute it with a flavour of your choice.

Ingredients

1 cup fresh grated coconut
½ cup fresh cream
2 tbsp. milk masala whey protein
A pinch of cardmom powder
1 tbsp. powdered almonds
1 tbsp. ghee
Sweetener to taste

Bringing everything together

1. Melt the ghee in a pan, add the grated coconut and cook for 3–4 minutes.

2. Add the cream, milk masala whey, powdered almonds, sweetener and cardamom powder.

3. Cook for a few minutes and bring everything together so all the ingredients are well-blended.

4. Take the mixture off the stove and let it cool for a few minutes.

5. Grease your palms, take a little mixture in your palms and make little balls or laddoos.

6. Repeat the process with the rest of the mixture and refrigerate the laddoos.

7. Consume them as per your macros.

Nutritional Information Per Serving

Serving Size – 3

Amount Per Serving

Calories 256

Total Fat 20 g

Total Carbohydrate 10 g

Protein 8 g

Get additional bonus material and access to a 7-day challenge by signing up at https://www.ketomonk.com/bonus.

Keto Chocolate Chikki

Generally, jaggery and sugar are used as the base for chikkis but this recipe requires unsweetened chocolate as the base.

Ingredients

200 gms dark unsweetened chocolate
100 gms butter
50 gms chopped nuts (almonds and walnuts)
½ tsp. sea salt
Sweetener to taste

Bringing everything together

1. In a microwave safe bowl, melt the chocolate with butter for three thirty-second intervals or till the butter and chocolate are completely melted and can be blended together.

2. Add the sweetner and chopped nuts and mix well.

3. Put parchment paper on a tray and spread the mixture evenly on it. Sprinkle with sea salt.

4. Place the tray in the refrigerator for a couple of hours or in the freezer for half an hour or more till it is set.

5. You can cut them into shapes of your preference.

Nutritional Information Per Serving
Serving Size – 4

Amount Per Serving
Calories 507
Total Fat 54 g
Total Carbohydrate 15 g
Protein 10 g

Index

NOTES

NOTES

NOTES

NOTES

Made in the USA
Middletown, DE
18 October 2020

22307773R00113